TPBA | Play-Based | TPBI
TPBC

Read, Play, and Learn!
Storybook Activities for Young Children

Module
9

This is one module of a total collection of eight. The following are the other seven modules included in Collection 2:

Module 10: *First Flight*
Module 11: *Friends*
Module 12: *The Three Billy Goats Gruff*
Module 13: *The Three Little Javelinas*
Module 14: *A Rainbow of Friends*
Module 15: *Franklin Has a Sleepover*
Module 16: *The Rainbow Fish*

In addition, there is a Collection 1 of **Read, Play, and Learn!** The following are the eight modules included:

Module 1: *The Kissing Hand*
Module 2: *Somebody and the Three Blairs*
Module 3: *Picking Apples & Pumpkins*
Module 4: *The Little Old Lady Who Was Not Afraid of Anything*
Module 5: *The Knight and the Dragon*
Module 6: *Abiyoyo*
Module 7: *Night Tree*
Module 8: *The Snowy Day*

Other products available in the ⌜TPBA⌐ *Play-Based* ⌐TPBI⌝ / ⌊TPBC⌋ system include the following:

- *Teacher's Guide for Read, Play, and Learn! Storybook Activities for Young Children*
- *Transdisciplinary Play-Based Assessment: A Functional Approach to Working with Young Children, Revised Edition*
- *Transdisciplinary Play-Based Intervention: Guidelines for Developing Meaningful Curricula for Young Children*
- *And You Thought They Were Just Playing: Transdisciplinary Play-Based Assessment* (videotape)
- *Observing Kassandra: A Transdisciplinary Play-Based Assessment of a Child with Severe Disabilities* (videotape)

Look inside the back cover for ordering information.

·P A U L·H·
BROOKES
PUBLISHING C^O

Baltimore · London · Toronto · Sydney

The Transdisciplinary Play-Based Curriculum from Toni Linder

Read, Play, and Learn!
Storybook Activities for Young Children

Module 9

Based on **A Porcupine Named Fluffy**

Module developed by
Toni W. Linder

This module was field-tested and reviewed by Regina "Patsy" Boughan, Katie Greer, and Karen T. Harmon.

Paul H. Brookes Publishing Co.
Post Office Box 10624
Baltimore, Maryland 21285-0624

www.brookespublishing.com

Typeset by A.W. Bennett, Inc., Hartland, Vermont.
Manufactured in the United States of America by
Printing Corporation of America, Baltimore, Maryland.

This curriculum contains activities and suggestions that should be used in the classroom or other settings *only* when children are receiving proper supervision. It is the teacher's or caregiver's responsibility to provide a safe, secure environment for all children and to know each child's individual circumstances (e.g., allergies to food or other substances, medical needs). The authors and publisher disclaim any liability arising directly or indirectly from the use of this book.

For information about Toni W. Linder, Ed.D., and the module developers, please refer to pages vii–viii of the *Teacher's Guide for Read, Play, and Learn! Storybook Activities for Young Children.*

1-55766-411-0

CONTENTS

HOW TO USE *READ, PLAY, AND LEARN!*

Think how much more motivated to read children would be if reading stories and using print materials enriched and enlivened their play. The booklet you are holding in your hands is one of several modules in *Read, Play, and Learn!*, a play-based curriculum designed not only to enhance emergent literacy skills but also to promote growth across all of the areas of development important for a young child.

The Curriculum

A storybook-based curriculum is not a new concept. Teachers and child care providers have, after all, been using books as an important piece of their programming for centuries. What is different about this curriculum is the integration of all areas of development into a full spectrum of activities, all relating to one book, with accompanying modifications and adaptations to meet the needs of *all* children in the class. *Read, Play, and Learn!* encourages children to *actively participate* in a *literacy-rich* environment of *playful* activities that foster *cognitive, language, social,* and *motor* development.

Module Format

Each module of *Read, Play, and Learn!*, using the magic of a different storybook, provides 2 weeks of engaging, theme-based activities to help children learn. This module, like all of the others, has the following sections:

1. *The Story:* A brief retelling or summary of the picture book, with information on where to get the book
2. *The Planning Sheets:* Charts for at-a-glance reference to all of the suggested activities to use for the 2 weeks
3. *Vocabulary:* A list of the key words and concepts, including labels, action words, and descriptors, to which the children can be introduced with this story
4. *Materials:* A list of the toys, playthings, equipment, supplies, food, and other items needed for the module
5. *Areas/Centers:* A description of 10 days of different activities for each area or center in the classroom, plus suggested modifications for the sensorimotor, functional, and symbolic levels of learning (described in the next section)
6. *How to Involve Families:* Recommendations to help keep family members or other caregivers informed, including sample letters to send home
7. *More Suggestions:* Alternative storybooks and other activities (e.g., songs, fingerplays, resources, software) that can be used with the module

In most instances, you will probably find there are more activities than you will use. This overplanning is intentional so that you can select activities that match the interests, abilities, and educational and developmental needs of the children you serve.

The Play Areas

The "centers," or areas of the classroom, include places for reading the story, dramatizing the story, and engaging in sensory and motor play; a literacy center; an art area; and sites for science and math activities, floor play, table play, outdoor fun, woodworking, and snacktime. The centers may be distinct or may serve multiple purposes. All centers may be set up in the room simultaneously, or you may choose to generate only a few of the areas at a time. Adding to or changing the centers for each of the modules to maintain children's high level of involvement is encouraged. For more background on structuring your classroom, refer to the *Teacher's Guide*.

The Teacher's Guide

Be sure to read the ***Read, Play, and Learn!*** *Teacher's Guide* before using any of the modules. (If you do not already have your copy, ordering information is included on page 74.) The *Teacher's Guide* describes the foundations of the curriculum, provides instruction in using the curriculum with children of different ages and ability levels, offers suggestions for classroom set-up, reviews the stages of literacy development, and helps you get family members or other caregivers involved. You will also find helpful information on weekly planning, team use of the modules, and sequencing of modules to correspond with holidays and seasons of the year.

The Children

Read, Play, and Learn! has been designed primarily for children between the ages of 3 and 6. You will find it effective, though, with children in your classroom whose developmental age ranges from 1 to 6 years old. As you progress through each module, you will find that levels of learning are discussed for the activities in each play area or center. By following the tips in these sections, you can adjust the suggested activities to the needs of the individual learners in your classroom. The *Teacher's Guide* and other products from Toni Linder (1993a, 1993b) will help you learn to identify the level of learning for which each child is ready.

1. *Sensorimotor:* At this earliest level of development, children are learning about concrete meanings through physical manipulation of the environment around them. They are more interested in the sounds of words being read, pictures in a book, and the concrete associations of the words that are meaningful to them. This stage roughly corresponds to the cognitive and language levels of children functioning from early infancy to about 18 months of age. This stage is also called the *exploratory* level.
2. *Functional:* At this second level, children are listening and watching, imitating, relating, and beginning to sequence ideas and actions. They are interested in listening to the story but are still more interested in talking about the pictures than telling the story per se. This level coincides approximately with children functioning from about 18 months to 3 years of age.
3. *Symbolic:* When children become interested in learning and representing their understanding through a variety of representational and symbolic

means, including fantasy play, storytelling, music, dance, art, drawing, and print, they have reached the symbolic level. Children at this level, typically 3 years of age or older, become interested in the print in the picture book, the story sequence, and the telling of the story.

Why Should I Use Read, Play, and Learn!? The advantages of **Read, Play, and Learn!** are many. The use of the same storybook over 2 weeks (it can be extended to a longer period of time if desired) allows repeated encounters with themes and concepts and the modification, adaptation, and generalization of skills related to those ideas across time and from school to home. The reiteration of concepts and themes provides opportunities for understanding in multiple ways. The development of projects allows children to work at their own pace. Repeated exposure to activities builds memory skills. Actions, events, characters, language structures, and vocabulary are increasingly understood, retained, and applied. In short, each story, and its related activities, serves as the stimulus for discussion, play, exploration, investigation, dramatization, creative expression, socialization, and emerging literacy development.

Now, to Get Started . . . You will first want to familiarize yourself with the content of the *Teacher's Guide* and several of the modules. Then, choose a sequence of modules that makes the most sense for the time of year you are starting to use the curriculum and the children with whom you are working.

Read through the complete module. If you do not already have a copy of the storybook, obtain one. Each story associated with a module is a popular children's book available in most bookstores and libraries, but if you are not able to find the exact book, at the back of the module you will find a list of other books that you can substitute.

Refer to the Planning Sheets to see how the storybook becomes the basis for each day's activities. Then, gather the materials you will need, and plan how you want to set up your classroom. Everything you will need is identified in the Materials section of the module.

Now you are ready to use the daily suggestions in the areas/centers of the module to make **Read, Play, and Learn!** work in your classroom or child care center. The *Teacher's Guide* will give you more information on the importance of starting each day with the reading of the story followed by an acting out or dramatization. Each day you will embellish the reading and involve the children more; ideas for how to do this across the 2 weeks are included in the module. Then you can choose from among the many descriptions of specific activities for each area or center you set up. You may follow the Planning Sheets exactly or you may use the Planning Sheet Master in the Appendix at the end of the *Teacher's Guide* to modify and adapt the storybook modules for the children in your classroom. Each of these sections of the module is followed by tips on how to modify the activities so that all children benefit whether they are sensorimotor, functional, or symbolic learners. You'll be able to teach or supervise children in groups but still individualize the instruction to suit each child.

The *Teacher's Guide* includes suggestions for adaptations and modifications to use the curriculum with children with disabilities or special needs. By using

Read, Play, and Learn! in conjunction with Toni Linder's other products, *Transdisciplinary Play-Based Assessment* and *Transdisciplinary Play-Based Intervention* (1993a, 1993b), you'll make your classroom an inclusive learning environment. (To order either of these books, with more information on individualized family service plans and individualized education programs, refer to page 74.)

Before you are actually under way, be sure to read the important section on involving families. You'll want to let the care providers of the children you see each day know which story is being discussed in school so that learning can extend to the home. By sending home a letter of explanation and perhaps even a modified version of the Planning Sheets for the story, parents can work on vocabulary, themes, and concepts at home. The more parents know about what is happening during the day, the more they will have to talk about with their children. Some families will even go to the library or bookstore to have a copy of the storybook at home.

Have Fun! So, turn your classroom into a place for dialogue, discourse, and discovery, not just question and response. Modify and create; inspire and stimulate. Have fun, and the children you teach or care for will, too!

References

Linder, T.W. (1993a). *Transdisciplinary play-based assessment: A functional approach to working with young children* (Rev. ed.). Baltimore: Paul H. Brookes Publishing Co.

Linder, T.W. (1993b). *Transdisciplinary play-based intervention: Guidelines for developing a meaningful curriculum for young children*. Baltimore: Paul H. Brookes Publishing Co.

THE STORY

A Porcupine Named Fluffy, written by Helen Lester and illustrated by Lynn Munsinger, is a delightful tale of a young porcupine who wants to live up to his name. Fluffy's parents choose the name Fluffy because it is a pretty name, but Fluffy discovers that he is not at all fluffy and goes about trying various means to become fluffy. He tries to "be" a cloud and a pillow. He experiments with a bubble bath, whipped cream, marshmallows, shaving cream and feathers, and even a bunny outfit, but nothing works. He is very dejected and becomes greatly embarrassed when he runs into a rhinoceros who teases him and laughs at his name. But after Fluffy discovers that the rhinoceros is named Hippo, he laughs as well, and the two become fast friends.

This story provides numerous opportunities for sensory experiences as well as the development of descriptive concepts and expression of feelings in dramatic play. Opportunities abound for cognitive, social-emotional, language and communication, and sensorimotor experiences for children of all ability levels. The ideas that follow are merely samples of activities that can be done with this story.

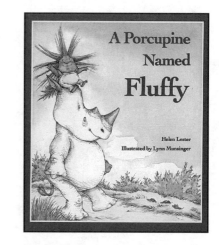

Title:	*A Porcupine Named Fluffy*
Author:	Helen Lester
Illustrator:	Lynn Munsinger
Publisher:	Houghton Mifflin Company
Price:	$5.95*

Try your local bookstore or library to obtain this book.
*Suggested retail price

Play-Based Curriculum Planning Sheet: Storybook Activities

Date: Week One   **Theme (optional):** Friendship   **Book title (optional):** A Porcupine Named Fluffy

Play area	Monday	Tuesday	Wednesday	Thursday	Friday
Reading the Story	Read the story using a variety of props and dramatizing several sections. Introduce the key characters and concepts.	Read the story again, but this time leave out key words. Children participate in telling the story by "reading" the pictures.	Before turning the pages of the book, have the children predict what is going to happen next. The children describe the pictures.	Read one page of the story, and have a child "read" the next page.	Let the children take turns telling the story. Assist some of the children in acting out various scenarios.
Dramatic Play: Theme Area	Role-play the story. Let all of the children see the team, and have a few peers enact the selected events. Provide a script.	The story is enacted by several children who choose to dramatize the story. You can assist with suggestions and prompts.	You can take a less active role with children who have been acting out the story. Written cue cards or picture cards can be used to prompt.	Prompts are reduced, but you may want to add creative suggestions for introducing an additional story event.	Many of the children will have mastered several of the events in the story and will need little prompting. Embellishment and improvisation can take over.
Literacy Center	Have the book and tape available. Children can make labels and signs. Letter and animal stamps and stamp pads can be used.	Have the book and tape available. Write letters to Fluffy. Children can make and cut out labels for the sensory tubs.	Have the book and tape available. Children can dictate a story to you about the pictures selected the previous day. Make labels for the mural.	Have the book and tape available. Continue with story dictation. You may prompt more descriptions or actions.	Have the book and tape available. The children can describe what they see on the mural. They can then dictate a story about the mural.
Science and Math Center	Experiment with different objects to determine which things stick together. Create a chart. Begin the potato porcupine experiment.	Continue with the experiments on what sticks together. Check on the potato porcupines. Generate questions about porcupines.	Add more objects and materials to the potato experiment. Check on the potatoes. Have references available with pictures and information.	Play a computer game. Experiment with bubble wrap and pencils. Check on the potatoes.	Repeat the measurement activities. Start to work on the Fluffy and Hippo game. Check and measure the potato porcupines.
Art Area	Begin a mural. Have the children paint the blue sky and green grass.	Continue on the mural. Children can paint clouds in the sky or glue on stretched-out cotton balls.	Have the children glue their sandpaper porcupines onto the mural. Label with their names. Set up the easel with chalk.	Children can glue their sponge hippos onto the mural. Set up the easel with markers.	Children can add houses, a path, rocks, or whatever they want to the mural. Labels made by the children in the Literacy Center can be added.
Sensory Area	Make shaving cream paintings. Explore sensory tubs of warm water, shaving cream, and wood chips.	Explore one sensory tub filled with cotton balls, foam rubber pieces, and Koosh balls and another that is filled with bobby pins.	Fill a tub with warm water and a tub with utensils. Have the children add bubble bath and food coloring to the water and use the utensils to make bubbles.	Fill sensory tubs with water and dry sand. The children can make sand porcupines.	Make slime in the tubs. Add plastic animals to try to make them "Fluffy."
Motor Area	A straight path is made of two strips of masking tape. The children can walk down the path and then roll around on the mat laughing.	A rope is used to make a curved path on which the children can walk.	Make a path from strips of bubble wrap laid out in geometric shapes on which the children can jump or hop.	Cut out paper circles, triangles, and squares, and place them on the floor in a pattern. The children jump from circle to circle.	Rearrange the shapes from the previous day so that the children can step or jump from square to square.

From *Read, Play, and Learn!* by Toni W. Linder © 1999 by Paul H. Brookes Publishing Co., Inc.

Play-Based Curriculum Planning Sheet: Storybook Activities

Date: Week One   **Theme (optional):** Friendship   **Book title (optional):** A Porcupine Named Fluffy

Play area	Monday	Tuesday	Wednesday	Thursday	Friday
Floor Play	A miniature scenario is placed on the floor. Place out puzzles of animals and put hedgehogs and Koosh balls in a bucket.	Children build trees from blocks and add cotton balls to make clouds on top of trees. Place out the hedgehog toys and Koosh balls.	Build paths around the "cloud trees" using blocks, bubble wrap, or paper strips. Place a wire maze on the floor.	Add the clay or sponge porcupines and hippos made during Table Play to the miniature scenario.	Repeat the miniature scenario. Add marshmallows and shaving cream. Place out switch toys and books and puzzles.
Table Play	Children can make sandpaper porcupines. Play the Silly Faces Colorform game.	Children can make sponge hippos or rhinoceroses. Continue to make sandpaper porcupines. Repeat the Silly Faces Colorform game.	The children make clay Porcupine families. Continue to make sponge hippos.	Children make Styrofoam animal characters. Have children name their characters. Continue to make clay porcupines.	Repeat the previous day's activity. Talk about how the animals walk, what they eat, and who their friends are.
Woodworking Center	Children can experiment with putting different size nails and screws into wood and Styrofoam.	Children can continue to experiment with screws and nails. Some children may choose to make a bed for Fluffy out of wood and nails.	Children continue to make a bed for Fluffy out of wood or Styrofoam.	Children continue working on Fluffy's bed. They can make the mattress and the cover.	Children finish Fluffy's bed. They can paint the bed and add Fluffy.
Outdoor Play	Play Red Rover, Red Rover, We Want Fluffy to Come Over. Free play.	Children look for "hard" objects on a nature walk. Free Play.	Take another nature walk. Have the children look for soft objects on this nature walk. Free Play.	Give some children umbrellas and some children spray bottles. Children with the bottles go after the others with the umbrellas. Free play.	Go for a walk to look for pine cones or other prickly things. Free Play.
Snack	Oral motor: Have the children make "soft" and "hard" sounds. Snack: Soft and prickly "porcupines" and juice	Oral motor: Children choose their favorite animal sound to make; others imitate. Snack: Trail mix and water	Oral motor: Children wash their hands and face with rough, wet washcloths. Snack: Bananas and carrots and milk	Oral motor: Children can choose their favorite animal and make the noise the animal makes. Snack: Celery with peanut butter and juice	Oral motor: Sing "Did You Ever See a Porcupine?" Snack: Granola and whipped cream and water
Books and Music					
Software					

TPBA   Play-Based   TPBI

TPBC

From *Read, Play, and Learn!* by Toni W. Linder © 1999 by Paul H. Brookes Publishing Co., Inc.

Play-Based Curriculum Planning Sheet: Storybook Activities

Date: Week Two   **Theme (optional):** Friendship   **Book title (optional):** A Porcupine Named Fluffy

Play area	Monday	Tuesday	Wednesday	Thursday	Friday
Reading the Story	Read the story again. Discuss feelings of sadness and embarrassment, teasing, and hurt feelings.	One child "reads" the story with you while the other children act out feelings. The children begin to share their artwork, center experiences, and findings.	Children "read" the story, label pictures, or demonstrate a part. Give each child a cotton ball to hold up every time the word "Fluffy" is read.	Read the story again. Sing "One Little, Two Little, Three Little Porcupines." The children continue to share information.	You and the children read the story together and act out various parts.
Dramatic Play: Theme Area	Repeat the dramatization. You can now add new vocabulary or "lines" to the script, as well as new props.	The story can be expanded to add new actions when Fluffy meets Hippo (e.g., hugging, shaking hands).	Let the children make up what happens next after they role-play the script. "Read" the letters left in the mailbox.	Let the children continue to dramatize the story. Minimal facilitation is needed. Encourage them to add to the script.	Let the children continue to dramatize the story.
Literacy Center	Have the book and tape available. At the writing table, the children can search for and cut out pictures from magazines.	Have the book and tape available. Children choose a picture from the second fifth of the book. Have children talk about the pictures, and write down their words. Write letters.	Have the book and tape available. Choose pictures from the third fifth of the book. Same as the previous day.	Have the book and tape available. Choose pictures from the fourth fifth of the book. Same as the previous day.	Have the book and tape available. Choose pictures from the last fifth of the book. Same as the previous day.
Science and Math Center	Work on the Fluffy and Hippo game. Compare hard and soft items. Compare a hard-boiled egg with a raw egg.	Play the Fluffy and Hippo game. Experiment with changing something from hard to soft. Measure the potato porcupines. Chart the results.	Teach the Fluffy and Hippo game to a peer. Measure the potato porcupines. Continue experimenting with soft and hard things.	Experiment with making things fluffy. Make whipped cream. Check and measure the potato porcupines. Chart the growth.	Play a computer game. Check and measure the potato porcupines, and chart the results. The children can draw faces on their potato porcupines.
Art Area	Make Fluffy bubble paintings. Make a picture chart for the children to follow.	Make patterns on paper using a variety of soft and hard objects. Repeat the bubble paintings.	Repeat the object painting. Make potato prints.	Repeat the potato prints. Make wrapping paper.	The children make sponge prints of porcupines on paper.
Sensory Area	Fill the wading pool with soft objects and 20 pictures. Have the children "dive" in and find the pictures. Play the Blue's Clues—Big Easy Game.	Let the children experiment with dry, uncooked spaghetti and cooked spaghetti. Repeat Blue's Clues—Big Easy Game.	Have the children slide in the slime on a mat. Play Elefun.	Let the children toss soft things into a tub labeled "soft" and hard things into a tub labeled "hard." Repeating playing Elefun.	Let the children try to pick up wet Corn Flakes in one tub and pine cones in another tub. Play the Blue's Clues—Big Easy Game.
Motor Area	Place a small ladder on the floor for the path. Children step in the spaces between the rungs, walk on the rungs, and so forth.	Create a path with obstacles (e.g., chairs, traffic cones). Children ride a tricycle down the path.	Draw numbers on several of the shapes made the previous week or on new shapes. Have the children step on the numbers in sequence down the path.	Children can use scooter boards to go down the path on their tummies or their bottoms.	Cut out paper circles—some blank and some with different letters on them. Have the children hop from letter to letter to spell "Fluffy."

From Read, Play, and Learn! by Toni W. Linder © 1999 by Paul H. Brookes Publishing Co., Inc.

TPBA   Play-Based   TPBI

TPBC

Play-Based Curriculum Planning Sheet: Storybook Activities

Date: _Week Two_   **Theme (optional):** _Friendship_   **Book title (optional):** _A Porcupine Named Fluffy_

Play area	Monday	Tuesday	Wednesday	Thursday	Friday
Floor Play	Repeat the miniature scenario. Play Hungry Hungry Hippos. Continue with the puzzles. Children explore sound jars.	Repeat the miniature scenario and all of the previous day's activities.	Bring out the miniature scenario again. Play Pick-Up Fluffy's Quills. Play with "porcupine" balls.	Mash potatoes with potato mashers. Hide the "porcupine" balls, and let the children find them by following the noise of the balls.	Repeat playing Hungry Hungry Hippos. Repeat the miniature scenario. Texture tubs can be added. Continue playing with the "porcupine" balls.
Table Play	Have the children bring in a shoebox from home. Assist them in cutting out a piece of felt to fit on the lid.	Have the children trace characters or anything they want from the story. Have the easel set up with paint.	Take the animals made from felt and have the children dip them in liquid starch and set them aside to dry. Have the easel set up with markers. Have out puzzles.	Let children act out the story with their own felt storyboard. The pieces can be placed inside to take home. Make pine cone porcupines.	Children can create clay or Play-Doh animals to which they can add pieces of pine cones, pipe cleaners, and so forth.
Woodworking Center	N/A	N/A	N/A	N/A	N/A
Outdoor Play	Go outside and hide the porcupines made by the children. Have the children find them. Free Play.	Set out a tricycle obstacle course. Some children maneuver this course, and some children play on the outdoor equipment. Free play.	Children move outside and inside the numbered circles. Play Fluffy Says. Free play.	Bring the ladder outside, and let the children walk through it in different ways. Play Fluffy, Fluffy, Hippo. Free play.	Bring big paper bag circles outside that were used for the path. Connect the big dots with dowels or sticks. Have the children follow the sticks.
Snack	Oral motor: "Make "soft" and "hard" sounds. Repeat "Did You Ever See a Porcupine?" Snack: Chocolate clouds and milk	Oral motor: Children wash their mouths with rough, wet cloths and dry them with soft, dry cloths. Do the Do This... fingerplay. Snack: Oatmeal and milk	Oral motor: Children make animal faces and sounds. Snack: Blender applesauce and apple juice	Oral motor: Do the Number Actions fingerplay. Snack: French fries and mashed potatoes with water	Oral motor: Children again choose from their favorite oral-motor activities and songs. Snack: Veggies and dip and milk
Books and Music					
Software					

From *Read, Play, and Learn!* by Toni W. Linder © 1999 by Paul H. Brookes Publishing Co., Inc.

TPBA *Play-Based* TPBC
Play-Based TPBI

VOCABULARY

Labels

Armadillos	Grass	Porcupine
Bubble bath	Head	Quills
Bubbles	Hedgehogs	Rhinoceros
Bunny	Hippopotamus	Rock
Clouds	House	Rules
Cotton balls	Meadow	Shaving cream
Door	Metal	Sponge
Egg	Miles	Tail
Field	Oatmeal	Tree
Flannel	Oats	Turtles
Forest	Opposite	Umbrella
Friends	Path	Velcro
Grain	Pillow	Wood

Action Words

Bang	Mash	Rub
Climbing	Pat	Shake
Crawl	Poke	Slide
Crying	Pound	Squeeze
Hop	Pour	Teasing
Jump	Push	Walk
Laugh	Roll	

Descriptors

Alike	First, second, third, and so forth	Sad
Beginning	Fluffy	Same
Big, biggest	Furry	Scratchy
Bubbly	Gooey	Sharp
Bumpy	Happy	Short
Cold	Hot	Slimy
Creamy	Hard, harder	Slippery
Crunchy	Hurt	Slow
Different	In	Small, smallest
Dry	Last	Smooth
Easy	Long, longer, longest	Soft
Embarrassed	Lumpy	Squishy
End	Out	Sticky
Equal	Prickly	Thick
Fast	Quiet	Thin, thinnest
Fat, fattest	Rough	Wet
		Yucky

MATERIALS

Toys and Equipment

Animal and letter stamps
Beanbags
Blender
Blocks
Blue's Clues—Big Easy Game
Board books
Board games with rules (e.g., "Hungry Hungry Hippos")
Bubbles and bubble wand
Couch or chairs (small)
Dollhouse
Double boiler
Easel
Electric hand mixer
Elefun
Gym mat

Hedgehog or other squeeze toys with little prongs
Jiggle Ball (battery-operated vibrating ball)
Koosh balls
Ladder
Marbles
Miniature zoo animals (including a rhinoceros and a porcupine or rubber hedgehog)
Pick-up-sticks
Plastic animals
Plastic tubs
Play-Doh
Poker chips

Polaroid camera and film
Puzzles of animals
Reference books
Scooter boards
Silly Faces Colorform game
Stuffed animals and/or puppets
Switch toys, particularly animals
Tape recorder
Tinker Toys
Tricycles
Vise
Wading pool
Wire maze with beads

Supplies

Angel hair (such as is used on Christmas trees)
Barrel
Belts
Binder clips
Blankets
Bobby pins
Bottle caps
Branches
Brushes
Bubble bath
Bubble wrap
Butcher paper
Buttons
Cans with slotted lids
Chalk
Chart paper
Chopsticks
Clay or Play-Doh
Cloth
Clothespins
Combs

Construction paper
Cotton balls
Crayons
Crepe-paper streamers
Crocheted vest or net t-shirt, like those used for sports
Cube-shaped box
Cups
Dowels
Dried beans
Envelopes
Erasers
Fabric
Fake fur pieces
Fastening rings
Feather boa or long, silky scarf
Feathers
Felt, flannel
Foam rubber pieces
Garden or tent stakes
Glue (regular and wood)

Googly eyes
Hammer
Hand mirror
Hand-held eggbeater
Hard hats and goggles (for the Woodworking Center)
Hole puncher
Jars (from baby food jars to larger size jars)
Liquid starch
Magazines and catalogs
Markers
Matting boards
Measuring tape
Nails
Newsprint
Nuts, bolts, and screws
Oak tagboard
Paintbrushes
Paints
Paper bags (large)
Paper clips

Pastry tube
Peeler (vegetable)
Pencils
Pennies
Pillows
Pine cones
Pipe cleaners
Plastic knives
Plastic sheets or place mats
Poster board
Potato masher (hand-held)
Prickly things, such as tooth-
  picks
Q-Tips
Rope
Rubber cement
Rulers
Safety pins

Sand
Sandpaper
Scissors
Screwdriver
Seeds
Shaving cream
Silverware
Slotted spoon
Sponges
Spools (empty)
Spray bottles
Stamp pads
Stapler
Sticks
Straws
Styrofoam balls and pieces
Tape (masking)
Tennis balls

Three-ring binders
Toilet paper tubes
Toothbrushes
Toothpicks
Towels
Traffic cones
Umbrellas
Utensils (e.g., fork, whisk,
  spoon, tongs, funnel,
  baster)
Velcro
Velcro board or felt board
Washcloths
Water balloons
Wood
Wood chips
Zippers

Food

Apples
Bananas
Beans
Butter
Carrots
Celery
Chocolate chips
Cinnamon
Coconut (shredded)
Cool Whip or whipping
  cream
Corn Flakes
Cornstarch
Eggs

Food coloring
French fries (frozen,
  microwavable)
Granola
Heavy cream
Instant mashed potatoes
Juice
Marshmallows, large and
  miniature
Milk
Noodles (cooked and
  uncooked)
Oatmeal
Peanut butter

Peanuts
Pine nuts
Potatoes
Powdered dip mix
Pretzel sticks
Oranges
Raisins
Rice
Salt
Sour cream
Sugar
Sunflower seeds
Vegetables for dipping
Yogurt

*See the sample ClickArt® at the end of the *Teacher's Guide*.

READING THE STORY

Day 1 Read the story using a variety of props and dramatizing several sections. The key characters, Fluffy and Hippo, are introduced; the concepts of *fluffy, soft, prickly, sad,* and *embarrassed* are explained. Use exaggerated facial expressions and intonation to capture the children's attention. Encourage the children to imitate the facial expressions associated with the various feelings.

Day 2 Read the story again, but this time leave out key words (e.g., "Fluffy wasn't . . . [fluffy]"). The children participate in telling the story by "reading" the pictures. See if the children can remember the facial expressions associated with the various feelings Fluffy had. Use a hand mirror to let children see their facial expressions.

Day 3 Before turning the pages of the book while reading the story, ask the children to predict what is going to happen next and what will be in the next picture. The children again describe the pictures. Individual children may act out what happens in certain pictures. Have some props from the story, such as a pillow and an umbrella, available to use. Compare the real object with the one in the picture.

Day 4 Read one page of the story, and have a child "read" the next. Take turns in this way, with different children assisting in the reading. Giving children this responsibility will encourage them to listen and anticipate what should come next. Active participation will also encourage the child who is "reading" to look closely at each picture for clues to what is happening.

Day 5 Let the children take turns telling the story by looking at the pictures. Assist some of the children in acting out the various scenarios with prompting.

Day 1 Read the story again. Discuss feelings of sadness and embarrassment, teasing, and hurt feelings. If you provide a pause at predictable places, the children will probably begin to jump in with words and phrases from the story. Have some toothpicks available for the children to touch and feel how a porcupine's quills are "sharp."

Day 2 One child "reads" the story with you while the other children act out feelings. Choose a child who can identify the actions in the story from looking at the pictures to assist with the reading. After reading the story, the children can begin to share their artwork, center experiences, and information they have learned from this module. A couple of children each day share so that the opening time can be kept short and hold everyone's attention.

Day 3   As you read the story, enlist the children to help "read," label pictures, or demonstrate a part. Give each child a cotton ball to hold up and squeeze every time the word "Fluffy" is said. Discuss activities during the past week and a half in which the children engaged that included things that were "fluffy." The children share information discovered in centers.

Day 4   Read the story again. Sing "One Little, Two Little, Three Little Porcupines" to the "Ten Little Indians" tune, counting the porcupines the children made during Table Play (Week 1, Day 1 and Day 3). The children continue to share information discovered in the centers.

Day 5   You and the children "read" the story together and act out various parts. The children should now be able to tell the story with little adult assistance. This initiative should be encouraged, even if the story "reading" is not entirely accurate!

Sensorimotor Level

1. The children at the sensorimotor level will enjoy seeing real objects paired with illustrations in the book. Emphasize the labels for familiar objects in the pictures, such as "pillow," "door," and so forth.
2. Use cotton balls to talk with these children about what "soft" means. The word "fluffy" can be used, as well; but this is a higher level concept, so children at this level will benefit most from the sensory experience of feeling the cotton ball and hearing the sound of the words associated with it. Emphasize touching and squeezing the cotton ball.
3. Emphasize familiar words for these children, and whenever possible, illustrate the word with an actual object.
4. Label the objects and characters in the pictures in the book, but *emphasize* the names for objects and people in the room. These are more concrete and meaningful to children at this level. For example, you can point out that Fluffy's face looks sad in the book, but the concept will be more meaningful if a peer shows these children a "sad" expression.

Functional Level

1. Have children at the functional level focus on simple sequences (e.g., becoming fluffy [put cotton on a toothpick to demonstrate]).

2. Show cause and effect (e.g., poke toothpicks through paper to illustrate quills) to these children.
3. Leave out key words in the story for these children to supply.
4. Label actions in pictures for these children. Children at this level are ready to look at the relationships among the various components of a picture (e.g., "Fluffy is crying. He is sad").

Symbolic Level

1. Children at the symbolic level can help "read" the story. For children who are aware that print tells the story, point out key words in print (e.g., "Fluffy").
2. Ask these children prediction questions (e.g., "What else will Fluffy try?").
3. Encourage children at this level to appreciate the humor in the illustrations. Ask them to describe why a certain picture is funny.
4. Encourage the children to do associational thinking. Talk about the names Fluffy's parents first picked. Why did they choose those names? Why is Fluffy a funny name for a porcupine?
5. Encourage divergent thinking. What else could Fluffy have done?
6. Talk about how friends usually have something in common. What did Fluffy and Hippo have in common? Who is your friend and what do you have in common?

DRAMATIC PLAY: THEME AREA

Dramatization of the story is done first by the team, with each part being exaggerated. The story can be enacted in both the House Area and in a theme area or "woods" or "field" where Fluffy encounters the rhinoceros named Hippo. The House Area is one end of the Dramatic Play: Theme Area, with a path through a "woods" to a "meadow," represented by a gym mat in the Motor Area. Have a mailbox with Fluffy's name on it so that the children can write letters to Fluffy. As the weeks progress and the children produce labels and props in the other centers, the materials will be added to this area.

Day 1

WEEK 1

Role-play the story. The events to be enacted may include the following: 1) Fluffy trying to become fluffy by wearing a pillow or putting cotton balls on his quills; 2) Fluffy meeting the rhinoceros and being sad and mad when the rhino laughs at him; and 3) Fluffy and Hippo falling down, rolling around, laughing at each other's names, and becoming friends. The children can then be assisted to act out the simple script. Children can be paired so that a child with the ability to remember the sequence can assist a child who needs some prompting. On the first day, not all children may have an opportunity to act out the story, but they will have the chance to see you, other team members, and possibly a few peers enact the selected events. The team may want to act out the story in the Dramatic Play: Theme Area for the children to observe, before the children choose the centers in which they want to participate. In this way, children will be encouraged to choose dramatic play and will have a model for actions if they return to this area later. The team can improvise with a script such as the following:

SCRIPT

Fluffy: I want to be fluffy. (Fluffy tries to be a pillow, and his mother sits on him.)
Mother: Ouch.
Fluffy: I'm not fluffy! I'm sad. (Fluffy walks down the path and meets Hippo.)
Hippo: What's your name?
Fluffy: Fluffy. (Hippo smiles, laughs, slaps his knee, and rolls on the floor.)
Fluffy: What's your name?
Hippo: H-H-Hippo. (Fluffy smiles, laughs, slaps his knee, and rolls on the floor. They roll on the ground together and hug.)

(This script can be modified depending on the children, but as the weeks progress, they will need less prompting. Improvisations and additions are encouraged.)

Day 2   The story is enacted by several children who choose to dramatize the story. You can assist with suggestions and prompts. Children who choose to come to this area will probably move to another center after a time, and new children can be integrated into the story. Children may also choose to add other elements of the story to their dramatic play. Prompt the children to notice and "read" the signs they made in the Literacy Center that are now posted in the Dramatic Play: Theme Area. They can also be encouraged to "deliver" mail to Fluffy from the Literacy Center. The mail can then be "read" by the children in the Dramatic Play: Theme Area.

Day 3   You can take a less active role with children who have been acting out the story. Written one-word cue cards or picture cards (e.g., "pillow," "path") can be used to prompt as is appropriate with individual children. These cards can help the child with picture–action association or word recognition with children at the symbolic level. With children at the sensorimotor or functional level, cue cards are not relevant, and modeling of actions and more adult support will be needed. (See the suggestions for the different levels at the end of this section.)

Day 4   Prompts are reduced, but you may want to add creative suggestions for introducing an additional story event for those children who have mastered the original sequence of events (for example, climbing a tree to try to become a cloud). In addition, the path is going to change every day (see the Sensory Area), so assistance in figuring out how to navigate the path may be needed. The focus in this area is to help the children, regardless of their level of cognitive development, and expand their ability to link ideas, actions, and interactions.

Day 5   By the fifth day, many of the children will have mastered several of the events in the story and will need little prompting. Embellishment and improvisation can take over. You may want to have an official "performance" with an audience.

Day 1   Repeat the dramatization. You can now add new vocabulary or "lines" to the script as well as new props. Add items that will reinforce the concepts of *fluffy* or *not fluffy*. For example, a feather boa, though not in the story, could be added to provide another "fluffy" prop.

WEEK 2

Day 2   The story can be expanded to add new actions when Fluffy meets Hippo. In addition to laughing, slapping thighs, and rolling on the ground, you can add hugging and shaking hands. Encourage the children to think about actions that show others that they like them. You might also introduce a few sign language phrases (e.g., DO YOU WANT TO PLAY? and I LIKE YOU).

Day 3   Let the children make up what happens next after they role-play the script. Encourage the use of phrases to indicate a desire for friendship. "Read" the letters written by Hippo that were left in the mailbox.

Day 4   Let the children continue to dramatize the story. Minimal facilitation is needed. Encourage them to add to the script. Become a "player," and let the children direct your actions.

Day 5   Let the children continue to dramatize the story. Minimal facilitation is needed. Let the children take turns performing for the rest of the group. All of the children can be involved in some way, as directors, performers, cue card holders, audience members, and so forth.

Sensorimotor Level

1. Let the children at the sensorimotor level explore the sensory aspects of the props (e.g., shaving cream, feathers, pillows).
2. For these children, label objects in the Dramatic Play: Theme Area and the actions that are being performed (e.g., "Fluffy is climbing the tree").
3. Help these children to participate in one or two actions (e.g., rolling on the mat) with peers. Describe for them what their peers are doing as they are doing it.
4. When the children at this level are observing others, facilitation is important. Point out what is happening, and give meaning to the actions they are seeing. These children are not yet at a level to understand role playing, so describe the actions and behaviors they are seeing.

Functional Level

1. For children at the functional level, facilitate the increase of the number of actions they can link into a sequence (e.g., find a belt and pillow, put it on, and look in mirror).
2. Concrete props are important for children at this level. For example, wearing fluffy or prickly vests and manipulating real objects, such as pillows or shaving cream, will remind the children of the story and motivate dramatic play.
3. Describe objects, actions, textures, and feelings for these children in order to add to their understanding of vocabulary.
4. Prompt these children to move to the next sequence of events in the story with the script, suggestions from a "director," or ideas from a peer model.

Symbolic Level

1. Involve the children at the symbolic level in planning and preparing the props and theme area.
2. Emphasize the humor in the story with these children. They will enjoy thinking of ways to make a peer laugh.
3. Generate new ideas for these children (e.g., "What else could Fluffy use to try to get fluffy?").
4. Present higher level concepts to these children: *opposites* (e.g., fluffy/prickly), *complex feelings* (embarrassment), and *incongruities* (a rhinoceros named Hippo).
5. Have these children act out the script in three to four events. Encourage children at this level to create additional dialogue for the dramatic play.
6. Encourage the children at this level to direct the dramatization of the story and extemporize the actions and words of the characters.
7. Encourage cooperative play with these children. They are ready to think about what goal they would like to accomplish and how they can involve others in reaching that goal.

LITERACY CENTER

Tape-record one of the team members (or a parent) reading *A Porcupine Named Fluffy*. The children may then come to this center and listen to and "read" the story again for themselves.

Day 1 Have the book and tape available for the children. Children at the symbolic level can help to make labels for the objects in the House Area: "Fluffy's quills" (where the vests are hanging), "pillows," "shaving cream," and so forth. Children who can copy letters and numbers can make road signs. One sign might point to the House Area and say, "FLUFFY'S HOUSE—2 MILES," and another at the other end of the path might say, "FOREST—3 MILES." Labels can be made for other centers as well. Children who are interested in making letters can invent their own forms, with you writing their meaning underneath. Some children may want to trace or copy letters. As the children form letters for a word, place a line under the word and say the word for the child. The line is a visual cue that the letters go together to make a word. Letter and animal stamps and stamp pads can be used by children who choose not to or who are unable to write letters. Let the children "read" what they have written to the other children.

Day 2 Have the book and tape available for the children. Children can make and cut out labels for the sensory tubs and objects in the Science and Math Center. Let the children who are interested write a letter to Fluffy. You may want to model this for the children by writing a brief letter and reading it aloud as you write. You can then ask who else wants to write a letter to Fluffy. They can choose to write it themselves, using their own "writing" style, or they can dictate it to you so that you can print it on paper. Let the children fold the letter, insert it in an envelope, stamp it, and deliver it to Fluffy's mailbox.

In addition, they can look through magazines for pictures of animals, cut them out, paste them down on paper, and dictate or write characteristics of the animals down on the paper, which you can then "translate." For instance, the children may find pictures of kittens, puppies, lambs, or other animals that are "fluffy," "soft," or "furry." Animals such as hedgehogs, armadillos, turtles, and so forth can have labels that describe them as "rough," "hard," or "prickly," as appropriate. Introduce and define the word "opposite," and use that word, whenever appropriate, to compare terms. Let the children name the animals and dictate their observations about the characteristics of the animals that they find for you to record. Label each page with the appropriate child's name. These pages can then be laminated and combined into a book called "Fluffy Animals and Hard or Prickly Animals" in a three-ring notebook for the children to look at and "read" over and over.

Day 3   Have the book and tape available for the children. Continue to write letters to Fluffy. Continue to add to the "Fluffy Animals and Hard or Prickly Animals" book. Make the book available for the children to examine and read.

The children can then dictate a story to you about some of the pictures selected the previous day. (Children can be encouraged to find "their" pictures and recognize their printed name on the page.) You may work with a group and use chart paper or with individual children on their own paper, depending on the level of the children and whether the goal is to make a co-operative story or to have each child think of his or her own story. If children dictate a story on an individual piece of paper, place the story in a page protector and add it to the notebook with the child's picture. The story may be as simple as an animal and an action or as complicated as a story about an animal that is unhappy about something. Children who are not interested in writing a story or who have been working on the mural in the Art Area may want to make labels for their contribution to the mural. You can assist as needed for the children's level of development.

Day 4   Have the book and tape available for the children. Continue with story dictation. You may prompt more descriptions or actions with questions (e.g., "Tell me about this animal . . . ," "What happened after he met the rhinoceros?").

Continue making labels and captions for the mural. Look at and read other books about hippos, rhinoceroses, and porcupines and animals that are sad, embarrassed, or different.

Day 5   Have the book and tape available for the children. The children who choose to come to this center can go to the mural in the Art Area, describe what they see on the mural, and "read" the labels that have been added. They can then go to the literacy table and dictate a story about the mural. These stories can be nicely mounted next to the mural.

Look at and read other books about animals that are sad, embarrassed, or different.

Continue to write letters to Fluffy.

Continue to add stories to the "Fluffy Animals and Hard or Prickly Animals" book.

Day 1   Have the book and tape available for the children. Pretend you are Hippo writing a letter to your new friend, Fluffy. The children can dictate a letter, either individually or as a group, that can then be addressed, stamped, and delivered to Fluffy's house.   **WEEK 2**

For the rest of this week, the children at this center will be retelling the story in their own words. Divide the book into five sections. (You can do up to five or six pictures per day or just select a few of the key pictures.) Prior to class, photocopy and laminate the separate pages of the book. For today, take the pictures from the first fifth of the book. Let the children each choose a picture and tell you the story about what is happening in the picture. Write down what each child says about his or her picture on a different piece of paper. (Keep in mind that some children may only label something in the picture. That is fine.) Read back to the child what has been said, and then let the child share the picture and "read" his or her writing to another child. Let the children decide in what order the pictures should be placed. What did Fluffy do first, next, and so forth? (The children may want to listen to the tape or look at the book to decide how to order the pages.) Hole-punch the pages of the laminated pictures and dictation pages and place them in a notebook in the order selected by the children. Read their story back to them.

At the writing table, the children can also search for and cut out pictures from magazines or catalogs of hard or prickly and soft or smooth things that might be in Fluffy's house. Have a variety of real soft, hard, and prickly objects in the center of the table, mounted on pieces of paper, and labeled. Have the children help you put them into groups of things that are alike. This is an activity to encourage grouping and classification as well as seeing the names of the objects in print. Assist the children by pointing out how the objects are alike or different. Children who cannot classify can still find and label the objects or the pictures for other children to group.

Look at and read other books about animals who are sad, embarrassed, or different.

Day 2
Have the book and tape available for the children. Take the laminated pages from the second fifth of the book, and let each child choose a picture to talk about. Write down their words. Add these pages to the notebook. Read the pages back to the children. The pictures of hard, soft, and prickly objects from the previous day can be glued onto paper, labeled with the name of the object and characteristics, and accumulated into a book, which can then be stapled together to take home. Let each child tell another child about his or her book.

Look at and read other books about rhinoceroses, hippos, and porcupines.

Continue to write letters from Hippo to Fluffy.

Day 3
Have the book and tape available for the children. Take the laminated pages from the third fifth of the book, and let each child choose a picture to talk about. Write down their words. Add these pages to the notebook. Read to the children what they have written. Some children may choose to write another ending to the story. What did Fluffy and Hippo do together after they became friends? Or what if they had not become friends? Read the story to them with the new ending. Which ending do they like better? Some children may prefer to look at and read other books about animals.

Look at and read other books about rhinoceroses, hippos, and porcupines.

Continue to write letters from Hippo to Fluffy.

Day 4
Have the book and tape available for the children. Take the laminated pages from the fourth fifth of the book, and let each child choose a picture to talk

about. Write down their words. Add these pages to the notebook. Read their evolving story to them.

Have the children find pictures in magazines or draw pictures of happy and sad people and animals. The children can then dictate to you or write (in their individual writing style) why the person or animal is happy or sad. You may write the children's meaning on the front or back of the picture.

Look at and read other books about rhinoceroses, hippos, and porcupines.

Continue to write letters from Hippo to Fluffy.

Day 5   Have the book and tape available for the children. Take the laminated pages from the last fifth of the book, and let each child choose a picture to talk about. Write down their words. Add these pages to the notebook.

Continue to label the pictures of emotions in animals and people. If there is time, staple the pictures into a book for the children to take home or laminate the pages and make a book to keep in the room to add to the bookshelf.

Sensorimotor Level

1. Children at the sensorimotor level will probably not choose this center. If they do, let them experiment with making marks on paper while the other children are trying to write or draw.
2. These children may enjoy having other children share the pictures in the books they are making.
3. Model for these children how to point to the pictures and label the pictures with simple words. This will help the children understand how to interact and communicate with children with less speech than they have.
4. Let these children study the pictures in the books and magazines. Have them name the objects or animals using simple words and phrases.
5. Have board books about animals for children at this level to examine.
6. Let these children try to make marks with stamps.
7. Encourage children at this level to listen to the audiotape.
8. Read simple animal books to these children.

Functional Level

1. Introduce children at the functional level to written labels (e.g., "fluffy," "soft," "porcupine"). This emphasizes to the children that you are making a separate mark for each word and there is a space between the words. Then, under those lines, write the words that the children said, saying the word as you write it. Finally, point to each word and underline it as you read it back to the children.

2. Introduce these children to the dictation of simple stories. Encourage the use of an object-action phrase (e.g., "Fluffy laughed").
3. Have these children use stamps with pictures to make labels or use letter stamps to make their names.
4. Label all of these children's artwork. Point out what you are writing so that the children will understand that print conveys meaning.
5. Encourage these children to explore printing as a means of telling people what they want to say. You can then build on their level of understanding.
6. Encourage children at this level to listen to the audiotape and try to follow along with the book.
7. Read simple animal action stories to the children at this level. Relate the animals to Fluffy and Hippo.

Symbolic Level

1. Encourage children at the symbolic level to make written labels for pictures and drawings (through picture or letter stamps, writing, or dictation). Help them to make comparisons and see the similarities and differences among the pictures, letters, and so forth.
2. Take exact dictations of the stories about these children's pictures, and encourage them to "read" their words to their peers.
3. The children at this level can make the labels for the centers and the props. Encourage them to use pictures and print in combination so that all of the children can understand the signs. Children may want to copy, trace, connect dots, or use other means to make letters and words.
4. Have these children make mileage signs for the path.
5. These children will enjoy using picture charts in centers and for snack. Make charts for them to follow for how to make their books. (For example, have a picture of scissors cutting out a picture, followed by a picture of a hand pasting the picture on a piece of paper, followed by a picture of a pencil writing a word next to the picture, followed by a picture of the completed page.)
6. Have these children label their work. You can take dictation or draw words for the children to trace or copy, depending on their ability and desire.
7. Encourage children at this level to expand their vocabulary concepts by adding new descriptors. For example, if the child describes a picture of a cloud as fluffy, you could say, "Yes, it does look fluffy. It also looks soft, like a giant pillow."
8. Have additional storybooks about animals available for children at this level.
9. Encourage children at this level to listen to the audiotape and read the story to a peer.

SCIENCE AND MATH CENTER

Day 1 Experiment with different objects to determine which things stick together. Show the children the picture of Fluffy stuck to the door with his quills. Tell them they can try different ways to make things stick like Fluffy did. Have a container full of different materials with which the children can experiment, such as paper, Velcro, wood, flannel, cloth, a zipper, glue, paper clips, a stapler, nails, screws, and tape. The children can make a chart on heavy oak tagboard with your help to show which materials stick together. Make a large grid with boxes down the side and across. In each of the boxes down the side, attach one of the items from the experimental pile. As the children experiment, they can place in the boxes next to that item the words, picture, or actual item that sticks to the item in the first box on the left. Use descriptive words about how the items hold things together. For example, in the first box, a piece of paper may be attached. As the children experiment, they can place the following items in the boxes next to the piece of paper—a dab of glue or the word "glue," a paper clip (or the words), a staple (or the word), a piece of tape (or the word), and so forth.

WEEK 1

    Begin the potato porcupine experiment. Take a close-up Polaroid picture of the potatoes you are using. Put old potatoes in a paper bag and wait for them to grow eyes (quills, in this case). Explain to the children that the potatoes will grow little sprouts that look a little like Fluffy's quills. Post the picture of the potatoes next to the bag of potatoes.

    If possible, borrow a hedgehog from someone so that the children can observe the spines and watch its behavior. A pet store may be willing to visit the classroom and show the children a hedgehog and demonstrate how the hedgehog is similar to a porcupine and how it is different. Unlike a porcupine, the children may be able to interact with a friendly hedgehog!

Day 2 Continue with the experiments on what sticks together. Add to the chart.

    Check on the potato porcupines. What is happening? Predict how many days it will take for the magic quills to appear.

    Prior to class, find reference books that have pictures and information about porcupines. Let the children generate questions about porcupines. Read the information to the children and try to find the answers to their questions. Discuss how books can help us answer our questions. If the class has an encyclopedia on the computer, the information may also be searched on the computer. This will enable children to see how computers can also give us answers to questions.

Day 3   Experiment with what else holds things together. Add new materials to the experiment, including safety pins, binder clips, and rubber cement.

Observe the potato porcupines.

Have reference books available with pictures and information about hippos and rhinoceroses. Let the children study the pictures and compare the two types of animals. How do they look alike? How are they different? Generate questions about the animals and look for the answers in the books or on the computer. Have pictures of a porcupine, a hippopotamus, and a rhinoceros on the wall in the Science and Math Center. As you find facts about each, write the facts under the appropriate picture, using the children's own words. Number each of the facts. Count the facts as you add to the list.

Day 4   Play a computer game, such as *Hello Kitty: Big Fun Shapes and Numbers*.

Experiment with bubble wrap and pencils. Explain how the bubbles are "fluffy" and full of air and the pencils are sharp, like Fluffy's quills. Try popping the bubbles with pencils and other tools, such as a finger, a fork, and so forth. See how hard the children need to push with a pencil to pop the bubbles.

Check on the potato porcupines. If "quills" have started to grow, measure them. Show the children how to look at a ruler and count the marks in between the inches. Let them experiment with measuring the length of lines on porcupines you have drawn and other straight objects. Some children may be ready for the words "short" and "long," whereas others will be able to count the increments on the ruler. Adapt the activity to the level of each child.

Have the reference books available for the children to study. Add to the list of facts under the three animals' pictures.

Day 5   Repeat the measurement activities for those who want to continue this practice. Let them measure other objects. Have several different quill-like objects out for the children to compare and measure. You might, for example, have a bobby pin, a toothpick, a chopstick, and a garden or tent stake. Help them compare lengths. Some children will be able to compare "big" and "small," others "long" and "short," whereas others can compare more than two items and use comparative terms such as "longer" and "longest." Use a ruler with marks and numbers only at the inch lines. (This can be made from a paint stir stick.) This will be less confusing for children who are just being introduced to numbers and measuring.

Start to make the Fluffy and Hippo game. In this game, the children will move their game pieces along a path composed of 1-inch colored circles and squares from Fluffy's house to the forest on the opposite side of the board. The children will design the board, arrange the shapes, and make the spinner. First the children can draw, trace, or cut out photocopied pictures from the book of Fluffy and Hippo. Let them attach these pictures to a piece of heavy poster board. Write the word "START" next to one of the pictures of Fluffy and the word "FINISH" next to one of the pictures of Hippo. The children can then cut out the squares and circles (or use squares and circles that are precut). Use three different colors of circles and three of the same colors of squares. Let the children create a path with the shapes on the board so they wind around from START to FINISH. Have them choose a shape and name the color and/or shape before they place it on the board next to the last one placed. Once the path is arranged so that the children are pleased, let them paste the shapes down on the poster board. (For children who recognize numbers, you can write the numbers from 1–6 repeatedly down the path.)

Check and measure the "quills" on the potato porcupines. Take another close-up picture of the potatoes and post it next to the first picture so that the children can see the change. Write the date the picture was taken under each picture.

Day 1 **WEEK 2**

Continue to work on the Fluffy and Hippo game. Prior to class, cover a cube-shaped box or a plastic cube from a set of stacking cubes with construction paper. Now the children can make a game die from the covered cube. Let them select a shape for each color and paste one on each side of the cube. Write one of the numbers from 1–6 on each face of the cube. Draw the equivalent number of dots under each number. Now the die should have a shape, a color, a number, and dots on each face. Some children will use the shape, some the colors, some the dots, and some the numbers to tell them how far to move their game piece. (A regular die with dots from 1–6 can also be used for children who recognize numbers.) Make game pieces out of bottle caps. Put a different color of Play-Doh inside each bottle cap, and stick pieces of broken toothpicks into the Play-Doh to make Fluffy game pieces. Now the game is ready to play. Let each child, in turn, roll the die and move his or her Fluffy game piece to the first circle or square (or number) on the board that matches the top of the die. Let the children choose which indicator (color, shape, dot, or number) they want to use to tell them where to move their piece. Smart (or lucky) ones will choose the indicator that takes them the farthest.

Discuss how Fluffy knew he was not fluffy. Compare hard and soft items. Compare a hard-boiled egg (prepared before class) with an uncooked egg. Let the children discuss and describe the shell on the outside of the egg. How are the eggs alike? Different? Predict whether they are hard or soft inside. Let the children break them open (over a bowl!) and see what is inside. They can then use a plastic knife to explore the two types of eggs. Discuss how cooking the egg made it hard. Compare the "hardness" of the uncooked egg, the cooked egg, and the shell of both eggs.

Day 2

Play the Fluffy and Hippo game. You can choose to play by color, shape, or number. Experiment with changing something from hard to soft: Examine oatmeal in its uncooked or "hard" state, and then add water and cook it in a microwave; examine a whole apple, and then peel it, cut it, put it in water, and cook it in a microwave. Discuss the changes that took place. Compare how cooking turned the "soft" egg "hard" and the "hard" apple "soft." Generate ideas of other things their families eat that start out hard or soft and are changed after they are cooked.

Measure the potato porcupines. Chart the results.

Day 3   Let those children who have played the Fluffy and Hippo game teach the game to a peer who has not yet played the game.

Measure the potato porcupines. Chart the results.

Continue the experiment with changing something from hard to soft: Peel potatoes, cut them into pieces, and cook them in a pot of boiling water (but not our friends the potato porcupines). Save them for use tomorrow.

Day 4   Repeat playing the Fluffy and Hippo game and teaching the game rules to a friend.

Experiment with making things fluffy. Make whipped cream using a picture chart to guide the actions. Talk about the characteristics of the heavy cream before it is whipped (e.g., it is "wet," it "pours," it is "smooth"). Describe how whipping the cream puts air into the cream and makes it "fluffy," "thick," and "soft." Let each child have an opportunity to mix the cream. You may want to try different methods, including a whisk, a hand-held eggbeater, and an electric mixer. (The hand beater is especially good for children who need to learn to use both hands together.) You can then compare terms such as "fast" and "slow" and "easy" and "hard." Have the children mash the boiled potatoes.

Check and measure potato porcupines. Chart the growth. Take another close-up picture of the potatoes and place it next to the other pictures. Write the date under the picture.

Day 5   Play a computer game, such as *Richard Scarry's Busy Town Reading*.

Check and measure the potato porcupines, and chart the results. The children can now draw faces on their potato porcupines with a marker and take them home. Take the pictures of the potatoes and mix them up. Then let the children arrange the pictures in the order of what happened to the potatoes. Take the pieces of paper with the dates written on them under the pictures and see if any of the children can put them in order. Talk about which picture was taken "first." Which is the "smallest" number? Which picture was taken "last"? Which is the "largest"?

Sensorimotor Level

1. Observation and exploration of some of the objects (Velcro, flannel) may be of interest to children at the sensorimotor level. Encourage them to feel the items and then put them in a container with a slot or hole in the top. This gives these children a two-step sequence of actions to do with the objects.

2. Children at this level can participate in the exploration of all of the hard and soft items. They may have fun breaking open the eggs. Label all items (e.g., "Egg. Amy, let's feel the egg"). Encourage children at this level to

explore in a variety of ways. For example, they can touch the eggs, poke them, roll them, stir the yolks, and so forth.

3. Children at this level will not understand the Fluffy and Hippo game, but they may enjoy putting round, colored poker chips in a can with a slotted lid.

4. Assist these children in pushing on the bubble wrap to make it pop. Let them try it with their fingers and a tool. Encourage them to make sounds (e.g., "pop!") to accompany their actions.

5. Children at this level can throw the die for their friends during the Fluffy and Hippo game.

6. Use adaptive equipment to make it easier for children at this level to make something happen on the computer. A simple game with animal pictures that can react with a simple touch of the key pad is appropriate for children at this level. This will enable them to see the effect of their actions.

Functional Level

1. All of the points mentioned for children at the sensorimotor level apply to children at the functional level as well.

2. Exploration of combining objects is appropriate for children at the functional level. They will love the Velcro and making things stick together with staples, glue, and paper clips.

3. Work with these children on problem solving in regard to making things stay together (e.g., using paper clips to put two pieces of paper together). Children at this level will have difficulty with paper clips, so use the large ones, and assist the children in seeing how the paper clip works. You may want these children to use a stapler, as it is easier to work and also provides an opportunity for children who need to develop increased tone and strength to push things.

4. Encourage these children to observe the potato porcupines. Have them tell what is happening. Encourage them to compare the changes with the potatoes in the pictures.

5. Children at this level can begin to understand making something happen on the computer. They may still benefit from an adapted keyboard.

6. Encourage turn taking on the board game. The children at this level may not understand the goal and sequence of the game, but you can prompt them to observe their peers, comment on what is happening, explain their turn, and label the parts of the game. They will enjoy moving their game piece but may not be able to move the piece the appropriate number of spaces without prompting. Encourage these children to match either colors or shapes. Matching both will be too difficult, as this requires the conceptualization of two attributes of an object at the same time.

7. Let children at this level find the picture of the potatoes at the "beginning" and the "end."

Symbolic Level

1. Children at the symbolic level can classify items into different categories of objects that hold things together (e.g., material, metal, sharp). Encourage the children to compare and contrast objects and look at the discrete parts.

2. Encourage these children to think about "why" something happens (e.g., the soft egg center gets hard, the air makes the cream fluffy) or "how" something works (e.g., the paper clip needs to spread apart at one end).

3. Set up situations in which the children have to use one-to-one correspondence or the ability to understand that one item directly relates to another (e.g., the gamepiece must move over a certain number of squares on the game board; each quill on the potato is different and may be a different length; each picture on a picture chart corresponds to an action we need to perform).

4. Have these children dictate results as you add to the charts. Involve the children in as many aspects of the chart making as possible.

5. Let these children make up rules to the Fluffy and Hippo game. The rules will probably change, but the idea of unchangeable rules is acquired slowly. Children at this level can begin by trying to state directions to another peer.

6. Encourage these children to identify color *and* shape (simultaneously) and to identify numbers on the Fluffy and Hippo game. You can make the game more difficult by adding more complex shapes or higher number concepts.

7. Increase these children's vocabulary by providing synonyms for words and explanations (e.g., "Gooey means that it is kind of wet and sticky"; "Oatmeal comes from a plant, a grain called oats").

ART AREA

Day 1
Begin a mural. On one wall in the room or out in the hall, place a large, long piece of butcher paper. Have the children paint with brushes and/or sponges a blue sky and green grass. (Remember that the children are doing this. If they do not paint the upper half blue for the sky and lower half green for the grass, that is okay. Do not expect perfection.)

Day 2
Continue working on the mural. Place scenic pictures with different types of clouds around the mural for the children to see. Encourage them to look out of the windows at the clouds in the sky. Talk about the different kinds of clouds and why they are fluffy. The children can then paint clouds in the sky on the mural or glue on clouds using rubber cement and stretched-out cotton balls or angel hair (the white, filmy material used at Halloween and Christmas) for clouds. The children may choose to use white paint or mix shades of gray with white and black paint.

Have the easel set up for painting the characters in the story (or some other story, if it strikes their fancy). Let the children try painting on the easel with Q-Tips or cotton balls in addition to brushes and sponges. Point out the differences in the effect when the different tools are used.

Day 3
Have the children glue their sandpaper porcupines (made at Table Play, Week 1, Day 1) onto the mural. Label their porcupines with their names. Some children may want to dictate to you what their porcupine is doing. Write their comments on pieces of paper to be attached to the mural near their porcupine.

Have the easel set up with chalk. White chalk may encourage the children to make more clouds, whereas brown chalk may inspire the drawing of the animals. Staple pieces of sandpaper over paintbrushes and let the children experiment with dipping the sandpaper brushes into paint and painting a design on paper.

Day 4
The children can glue their sponge hippos (made at Table Play, Week 1, Day 2) onto the mural. Talk about where on the mural the hippos should go. What is he doing? Again, write down the words the children say on a piece of paper to be attached to the mural. See if they can find their porcupines from the previous day, and see if they can remember what their words say. Read them the words they dictated.

Set up the easel with markers. Have photocopied pictures from the story next to the easel in case the children want to see a model for drawing these animals. You can facilitate by pointing out the shapes and lines of the ani-

Module 9 • 33

mals, the body parts, and so forth. The point is not to direct their drawing but to provide a reference, if needed or desired.

Day 5
The children can add paper or painted houses, a path, rocks, or whatever they feel should be included on the mural. The children who chose to make labels at the Literacy Center can add their labels, or you can write directly on the mural as the children dictate their captions. For some children, labeling the item is enough, whereas other children will be able to provide more of an explanation or description of the items they have added.

Day 1
Make fluffy bubble paintings. Have a photocopy of the picture of Fluffy in a tub next to a plastic tub of water. Make a picture chart of the following action sequence for the children to follow: 1) Add food coloring to the tub of water, 2) add bubble bath or dish soap, 3) give the children straws, and 4) let them blow with the straws into the water until lots of bubbles form. (If children suck instead of blow, adapt this activity and have them stir the bubbles instead.) Discuss how the bubbles are fluffy and compare them with the bubbles in the picture of Fluffy in the tub. 5) Let each child take a piece of construction paper and hold the paper above the bubbles, and 6) then *slowly and carefully* lower the paper until it touches the bubbles and leaves a print of the bubbles on the paper. Turn the paper over and look at the design left by the bubbles. Have the children put their names on their bubble paintings for display. (Translate unreadable markings.)

Day 2
Using a variety of soft objects (e.g., sponges, cloths, erasers, toothbrushes) and hard objects (e.g., wood, bolts, nuts, bottle caps), let the children experiment with dipping the objects into paint and making patterns on paper. Talk about the texture, color, and shape of the components of their design. Model using different materials to obtain different effects on the paper.

Repeat the bubble paintings.

Day 3
Repeat the object painting.

Make potato prints. Save some potatoes from the Science and Math Center. Cut a potato in half, and let the children press an object into the flesh of the potato using some of the hard objects from the previous day. Dip the marked end of the potato in paint, and make potato prints on paper. Compare these prints with the prints from the previous day. See if the children can recognize which objects made specific shapes. In

addition to being a fun art experience, this activity develops observation and comparison skills and is good for children who need to increase strength or who would benefit from activities requiring resistance. (See the section on facilitation of motor development in Chapter 4 of the *Teacher's Guide*.)

Day 4   Repeat the potato prints.

Make wrapping paper. The children can make wrapping paper by making designs on large pieces of newsprint with a "fluffy" feather dipped in paint. Then, using letter stamps, the children can stamp the letters or the word "F-L-U-F-F-Y" over and over on the paper. Provide a stamped model for the sequence of letters, but do not expect the children to be able to follow the sequence exactly. Some children will just stamp the letters, some will sequence one or two letters, and some may try the whole word. Take the opportunity to name the letters and make the letter sounds with the children as they are making them. When dry, this paper can then be used as wrapping paper to wrap the children's felt board theater boxes to take home. (See Table Play, Week 2.) The children may also want to stamp or decorate some writing paper to make stationery. You can then include a note (that the children help to compose) to tell the parents what the box is and that the stationery and wrapping paper are "hand-painted originals." You can also suggest that both felt board storytelling and making decorated paper might be fun activities to share with their child at home. Make sure that the children see you write the note and that you read them what it says. This will encourage some children to pretend to read the note to their parents when they get home.

Day 5   The children make sponge prints of porcupines on paper. Any oval or round sponge can be used to make the body of the porcupine. Quills can be added to the sponge painting by dipping toothpicks in paint and placing them flat on the paper on the top of the porcupine body. This is a good fine motor activity, as it requires prehension and careful placement of the toothpicks. A simpler way to make quills is to use "1" stamps around the body of the porcupine or "F" or "E" letter stamps placed sideways on top of the porcupine body. For children at the symbolic level, the letter stamps can be used again to spell out F-L-U-F-F-Y on the sponge painting.

Sensorimotor Level

1. For the children at the sensorimotor level, the goal is to experience the cause and effect of different media (e.g., crayons leave a mark), not to create a porcupine or a picture of some "thing."
2. Encourage these children to experiment with the objects, sponges, stamps, and so forth.
3. Label the body parts these children are using (e.g., "You are pushing with your *fingers*," "Touch your *face* with the sponge").

4. Children at this level may be more successful painting on a large surface while sitting on the floor with a paper taped to a wall or low surface. When seated at a table, make sure that the children's feet are on the floor or a stool so that they are more stable. Their efforts at fine motor control will be easier if they are sitting in a stable position.

5. Let the children at this level play with damp sponges. They may be more interested in playing with the sponge rather than painting with it. Show them how they can squeeze, twist, and pinch the sponges.

Functional Level

1. For children at the functional level, combining objects is the goal. You should encourage these children to see the art as representing something.

2. Label artwork for these children so that they can begin to associate print with meaningful labels.

3. Discuss with these children the materials you are using. Provide the name of the object ("bolt"), the word for the actions ("push"), and descriptive words ("hard").

4. You may help children at this level by drawing part of an object for them and then having them add other parts. For instance, you could draw a body of a porcupine, add a couple of quills, and prompt the children at this level to add more quills, eyes, feet, and so forth.

5. Encourage these children to use a variety of materials so that they learn the labels for the items and develop a broader repertoire of fine motor schemes. For example, holding a paintbrush, a marker, a sponge, and a piece of chalk all require different hand adaptations and movements.

6. Encourage children at this level to talk about their art to their friends. This will increase their ability to initiate a conversation and take turns in a dialogue as well as enable them to practice using the concepts they are acquiring. For example, after Mark has painted some white spots on the mural, you can facilitate interaction with a peer. "Look, Felicia, Mark painted some clouds. Mark, tell Felicia how you painted a cloud."

Symbolic Level

1. Products are important to children at the symbolic level, but their "Fluffies" and "Hippos" should be their own rendition.

2. Children at this level can be helped to increase their ability to represent what they want in many ways. They may benefit from seeing a picture of a porcupine or other animal they want to paint. This will remind them of the various aspects of the creature that they may want to include in the painting. The goal is not to have the child produce a predetermined outcome but to notice details and see how they relate to the whole.

3. Discuss with these children what tools might make something that resembles quills or the fat body of a hippo. Describe the characteristics with

the children, and relate those characteristics to other methods that might produce a similar result. Experiment with the various methods to see what works best. Encourage the children to discuss their findings.

4. On the mural, encourage these children to think about all of the elements of the story they could add to the mural. Let them look at the book and analyze the illustrations to get ideas for the mural.

5. Encourage these children to experiment with and analyze what happens when various colors are mixed.

6. Provide many ways of describing textures. For instance, sandpaper is not only scratchy, but it is also rough, prickly, and made from small, sharp pieces.

7. These children can be encouraged to demonstrate, describe, and take turns with their peers to increase cooperative effort.

SENSORY AREA

The first week involves several different types of sensory exploration in plastic tubs or dishwashing containers. These ideas will address a combination of gross motor, fine motor, and sensory development as well as communication and cognitive development. Additional ideas are also provided to increase the variety of experiences.

Day 1   Place three plastic tubs on the floor several feet apart. One tub has a can of shaving cream in it, the second tub contains warm water, and the third holds wood chips and hidden paintbrushes. Explain to those children who come to this center that they are going to experiment with things that feel "fluffy" and "prickly" like in the story. Let the children make shaving cream paintings on a plastic sheet or on a rubber or plastic place mat. Food coloring can be added to the shaving cream a few drops at a time, and the children can mix it in with their hands or with a spoon or fork. Use words like "soft," "smooth," "fluffy," "gooey," "creamy," and so forth to describe what they are feeling. (You can also do this activity so that you can model exploration and use of the terms.) After this exploration is exhausted, the shaving cream on the children's hands can be washed off in the second tub of water. As the children wash their hands, they can mix the shaving cream into the water. Describe the texture of the water as "smooth," "wet," "creamy," "bubbly," "quiet," and so forth. After drying off their hands with a "rough," "bumpy," "scratchy," or "soft" towel, the children can crawl over to the third tub on the floor. Here they will find a tub full of wood chips, at the bottom of which they will find a surprise—paintbrushes. You can discuss the texture of the wood chips compared with the shaving cream (e.g., "hard," "rough"), the bristles of the brushes (e.g., "smooth," "prickly"), and so forth. Now they can explore painting the wood chips with the colored shaving cream (brought over by you or retrieved by the children). They can then check later to see what happened to the shaving cream on the wood chips.

Day 2   Repeat the shaving cream activity from the previous day for those who did not get an opportunity to try it or for those who want to repeat it.

In addition to the previous sensory tubs, explore one sensory tub filled with cotton balls, foam rubber pieces, and Koosh balls and another filled with bobby pins. Let the children look for the fluffiest cotton ball in the one sensory tub and then carry it over in a spoon or with tongs to the other sensory tub filled with bobby pins. The children can then poke bobby pins into the cotton ball to make a porcupine. This can be repeated as many times as the children desire. The "porcupines" can be saved for use in other activities. This activity requires planning and eye–hand coordination.

Day 3 Put one of the sensory tubs filled with warm water on a child-size chair. The height of the chair will encourage the children to play on their knees (kneel stand). Place bubble bath and food coloring next to it. Place another tub several feet away on another child-size chair. In this tub, place all kinds of utensils, such as a hand-held eggbeater, a slotted spoon, a whisk, a funnel, a cup, a baster, straws, and so forth. The children will discover that when they add the bubble bath, nothing much happens. You can encourage the children to knee walk (see the Motor Area) between the tubs to get things they can use to mix the bubbles into the water to make it "fluffy."

Day 4 Fill two sensory tubs: one with water and one with dry sand. Place the sensory tubs several feet apart. Have the children carry the water over to the sand tub using cups or small buckets or other containers. Play together with the children and demonstrate how adding a little water to the sand makes it like clay. Show them how to make a mound like an animal body. With the addition of a few toothpicks on a mound of wet sand, the sand and water mixture can become sand porcupines. Have a reserve tub of sand ready in case the children add too much water. Use this opportunity to explore what happens to the sand and how it feels different. Describe the textures and shapes as you play.

Day 5 Have the children make slime using a picture chart:

SLIME

Equal parts of cornstarch and water
or
Equal parts of liquid starch and white glue
Food coloring
  Mix up cornstarch and water or liquid starch and white glue. Add food coloring. Refrigerate this mixture until ready to use.

Plastic animals can be added in an attempt to make them "fluffy." Describe the slime as "slippery," "gooey," "yucky," "wet," and so forth. Ask the children why the slime isn't "fluffy."

Day 1 Fill a plastic wading pool with soft objects, such as foam rubber pieces, cloth scraps, and torn newspaper. Add 20 pictures of different kinds of animals. Have the children "dive" in and try to find the pictures. As they find them, they can count them and sort them into animals that have soft or smooth skins and animals that have hard or rough skins. Name the animals and describe them as the children find them. Some children may be ready to classify animals as birds, fish, farm animals, wild animals, and so forth.

WEEK 2

Play Blue's Clues—Big Easy Game. This is a 10-foot square floor game. The children move their markers on a path through Blue's house. As they play, identify the items in the house that are "fluffy."

Day 2 Have dry, uncooked spaghetti in a package. Have the children open the package of spaghetti, remove it, and feel the prickly ends. Then they can break the spaghetti into pieces and put it into warm water in a sensory tub. They can feel it as it becomes sticky and keep checking it and feeling it as it becomes softer. In another tub, have cooked, drained spaghetti. Next to the tub, place the cotton ball and bobby pin porcupines made previously. Place small bowls or bottle caps in front of each. You can suggest to the children at this center that they can tear or cut the cold spaghetti, place it in the tiny containers, and pretend to "serve" the hungry porcupines. This activity is tactile but also requires fine motor and dramatic play skills. Some children will just enjoy playing in the spaghetti, whereas others will want to do the whole sequence of preparing the food for the porcupines. This is a messy activity, so place newspaper on the floor under the tubs to aid in clean-up.

Repeat playing the Blue's Clues—Big Easy Game.

Day 3 Take some of the slime the children made the previous week, and put it in the sensory tubs and place the rest of the slime on a mat. Have the children take off their shoes and socks and slide on the mat. This is best done by only one or two children at a time, as they are likely to slip and fall on the mat. This requires balance and coordination to remain standing, but the children seem to like the laughing and falling parts the best. You may want to have the children wear bathing suits or put on old clothes over their own clothing for this activity. (This will also allow them to practice dressing.) Some children may prefer to play with the slime in the tub. Add utensils for slime play.

As an alternative to the slime sliding, which some children may avoid, play Elefun. This is a game with an elephant that blows butterflies out of his trunk. The children then try to catch the butterflies with their nets. Talk about how the elephant is similar to a hippo and a rhino and how it is different. Feel the air coming out of the elephant's trunk. Describe the butterflies.

Day 4 Set up two tubs several feet apart. Place a sign saying "Soft" in front of one and a sign saying "Hard" in front of the other. Have the children stand behind a rope marker on the floor (which can be moved up or back for different children) and toss sponges, wet rags, beanbags, and other soft objects into the "soft" bucket and tennis balls, pieces of wood, pennies, and other hard items into the "hard" bucket. Counting can be added to keep track of how many hard and soft items you have. Some children will be able to determine which bucket they need to toss the item into, but others will need assistance to determine whether the object is hard or soft. For yet other children, the goal is just to name the object and try to toss it toward a tub.

Repeat playing Elefun.

Day 5 Place wet Corn Flakes in a tub and empty bowls beside the tub. Let the children try to pick up the Corn Flakes with clothespins, chopsticks, tongs, or other similar tools and place them in the bowls. For those with skilled fine motor control, you can encourage them to try to pick up just one Corn Flake. (It's not easy!) In another tub, place pine cones with the same tools. The children can experiment with and discuss the differences between the two types of materials. Which is easier? Why?

Blue's Clues—Big Easy Game includes a 4-foot-long floor puzzle of a house. Let the children put the puzzle together. Identify soft, fluffy items in the house.

Sensorimotor Level

1. For children at the sensorimotor level, allow exploration!
2. Combine objects with sensory materials (e.g., animals in shaving cream) for these children. This will encourage the children to use two hands together and to manipulate the objects and the slime, for example, together.
3. Encourage these children to use a variety of actions (e.g., squeezing, poking, blowing, tossing). Model these actions for them. You can make it a fun game of taking turns doing the various actions. Exaggerate your gestures and expressions to encourage these children to imitate their peers.
4. Label materials and actions for these children to increase receptive language and provide a language model.
5. When playing with the various textures, make sounds and noises to hold these children's interest and encourage imitation. For example, when playing with the hard spaghetti, say "crunch, crunch." When playing with the soft spaghetti, make slippery sounds or say "squish, squish."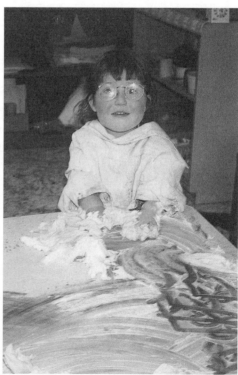
6. Pair children at this level with children who are exploring using different actions. These children will then provide a model.

Functional Level

1. The children at the functional level should be encouraged to combine actions (e.g., add food coloring to shaving cream). Try to prompt three to four different actions in a series before the child repeats his or her typical actions. For example, model stirring the shaving cream, then scooping some into a spoon, then dumping it into a container, and putting on a lid.

2. Add more complex actions (e.g., putting shaving cream in a toilet paper tube instead of a bowl) for these children.

3. Add more complex utensils (eggbeater, baster, pastry tube) so that the children will practice more sophisticated fine motor actions. These utensils will also promote problem solving as the children experiment with how to use them.

4. Encourage turn taking and conversation with these children. Children at this level may have difficulty maintaining a conversation. You can encourage communication by commenting on a child's actions and other children's actions. Avoid questions that only require a one-word response (e.g., "What color is that?"). Instead, use comments (e.g., "I wonder where that color came from," "Amy wants to know what to do with this").

5. Use action words and descriptive terms to increase these children's vocabulary comprehension and use (e.g., "Let's *poke* this slime. It is so *slippery!*").

Symbolic Level

1. Encourage higher level comparison and discrimination (e.g., different size bubbles) with the children at the symbolic level. Encourage them to compare the different types of materials they have explored.

2. Discuss the *how* and *why* of outcomes (e.g., "I wonder *why* this bubble is bigger") with these children.

3. Have these children predict (e.g., "What do you think will happen to the shaving cream in water?").

4. Encourage these children to ask questions about the materials and provide information to others (e.g., "Alex wants to know why noodles get soft").

5. Encourage these children to experiment with the more complex utensils. How many ways can they use each one? Prompt experimentation by saying, "I wonder what would happen if. . . ."

6. Pair these children with children who can benefit from a model using more sophisticated language and actions.

7. Children at the symbolic level can incorporate dramatic play into the sensory exploration. For example, you might suggest that the spaghetti is worms. Add some pipe cleaners to make hooks and try to get the worms on the hooks!

MOTOR AREA

Motor activities are planned for inclusion with the Dramatic Play: Theme Area and with the Sensory Area. Within the Dramatic Play: Theme Area, the path from the house to the mat will change frequently. Within the Sensory Area, the sensory tubs are placed on the floor, on chairs, and on tables so that the children are encouraged to scoot on their bottoms, crawl, or walk between them. Once at the tubs, children can be encouraged to play in various positions, depending on the height of the tubs and the motor needs of individual children. In this section, the motor activities for the Dramatic Play: Theme Area are described. In addition, the activities that are also taking place in the Sensory Area during the first 4 days of Week 1 are cross-referenced, as these activities also involve gross motor movements.

Day 1   Two strips of masking tape are used to make a straight path from the House Area to a mat in the Motor Area. The children can walk slow or fast down the path and then roll around on the mat laughing like Fluffy and Hippo at the end. Changing the pace of walking requires children to grade their movements, coordinating thinking and moving.

WEEK 1

   In the Sensory Area, the children are on their stomach or their hands and knees to play with shaving cream on plastic mats. This position requires shoulder strength and stability as well as good neck support. Children who need to increase tone, strength, and stability in the upper body can benefit from this position. In addition, the children are encouraged to move from one tub to another on their hands and knees. This movement is good for building shoulder and hip stability as well as the ability to use reciprocal movements while shifting weight from one side of the body to the other.

Day 2   A rope can be used to make a curved path. The children can walk down the path following the curve, using big and little steps, or placing one foot in front of the other. A barrel is placed on the mat so that the children can roll in it like Fluffy and Hippo rolled with laughter. Walking down the curved path with varying step sizes encourages children to use eye–foot coordination and to plan the placement of their bodies in space. Movement in the barrel provides vestibular stimulation and is an activity that is not only fun but also benefits children who need increased sensory input to raise their level of alertness or to raise their awareness of what is happening in their environment.

   In the Sensory Area, the tubs can be placed on tables, and tongs and spoons can be included so that the children can carry their cotton balls over to the next tub to combine with the bobby pins. This will require the children to combine eye–hand coordination with balance.

Day 3　Today the path is made from strips of bubble wrap laid out in a geometrically shaped path. The children can jump or hop down the path to the mat. Fluffy and Hippo get to roll in blankets on the mat. Jumping on the bubble path provides increased input to the joints and muscles (proprioceptive input) and helps children have a better awareness of body-in-space. Some children also need increased proprioceptive input to raise their level of awareness. Rolling in a blanket that is snugly wrapped around the child also provides deep pressure input that is pleasurable and calming to many children.

In the Sensory Area, the tubs can be placed on child-size chairs so that the children can be encouraged to knee walk between the tubs to get various utensils for their bubble experimentation. This activity is particularly appropriate for children who need to build hip stability.

Day 4　Cut out paper circles, squares, and triangles, and place them on the floor in a pattern so that the children can step or jump from circle to circle to get down the path. At the end, Fluffy and Hippo can roll and tickle each other. Rolling and tickling are means of providing both vestibular and tactile input, both of which are usually arousing to the system.

In the Sensory Area, the children can walk with full cups of water between the tubs. These activities address balance and eye–hand coordination.

Day 5　The shapes can be rearranged so that the children can jump or walk on the squares. They can roll in the bubble wrap (previously used for a path) at the end of the path on the mat. Rolling in the bubble wrap will provide intense sensory input to both vestibular and tactile systems.

Day 1　Place a small ladder on the floor for the path. Have the children, depending on their abilities, step in the holes between the rungs, walk on the rungs, walk with their feet outside the ladder, jump between the rungs, or cross it any other way that they can make up. This activity requires children to use reciprocal body movements (moving both sides of the body independently), to plan how to move their bodies through space, and to use balance and coordination. Repeat rolling in the barrel at the end of the path. Again, this provides vestibular and tactile input.

WEEK 2

Day 2　Make a path with obstacles (e.g., chairs, traffic cones). The children can ride a tricycle down the path around and through obstacles. This activity requires reciprocal leg movements, planning, and coordination. Repeat rolling in a blanket on the mat.

Day 3　Draw numbers on several of the shapes from Week 1, Days 4 and 5 or on new circles cut from paper, and place them on the floor so that children can step on the numbers in sequence down the path. Children who cannot recognize numbers can step on the ones with writing on them. Children can choose how they want to move to get to the next number. Repeat rolling in bubble wrap.

Day 4   The children can use scooter boards to go down the path on their tummies or on their bottoms. This requires reciprocal movement of the arms when the child is on the stomach, and reciprocal movement of the legs when seated on the scooter board. Both means require motor planning. Repeat rolling and tickling on the mat.

Day 5   Cut out paper circles, some blank and some containing the letters in the word "Fluffy," to place on the floor. Have the children hop from letter to letter to spell "Fluffy." You may prompt children with the letter, or, for children not yet at that level, just have them step on any letter or circle with writing. Several choices for rolling are placed on the mat (e.g., blanket, barrel, bubble wrap).

(*Note:* This area is not broken out by sensorimotor, functional, and symbolic levels. See Chapter 4 of the *Teacher's Guide* for discussion of individualizing activities for children with various types of motoric concerns.)

FLOOR PLAY

WEEK 1

Day 1 Begin working on a miniature scenario. Place the miniature scenario on the floor on a large piece of poster board to serve as a delineation of boundaries. Leave the scenario out over the course of the module so that the children can add to and modify it over time. Plastic animals (e.g., an infant's hedgehog squeeze toy can serve as a porcupine, a plastic rhinoceros from a set of zoo animals can serve as Hippo) are placed out next to a dollhouse (or the children can make a block house). The story can be reenacted with these characters, and the children can use blocks and other creative ideas to make a road, trees, and so forth.

In addition, place puzzles of animals out on the floor, and put Koosh balls and hedgehog squeeze toys in a bucket for squeezing, dropping, or throwing into a bucket or tub.

Day 2 The children can build "trees" or a forest out of blocks (any kind the children can manipulate, which may vary for individual children) to add to the scenario. Then they can put cotton ball clouds (pulled apart to look more like clouds) or angel hair (such as that used at Halloween as spider webs) stretched out over the top of the trees. Leave the tree structures up for play the following day.

In addition to the scenario, animal switch toys may be placed on the floor for those children at the sensorimotor level who are learning about cause and effect. (Actually, all of the children like the switch toys.) Place Koosh balls and hedgehogs out again with a target, such as blocks stacked up into tall "trees."

Day 3 Build paths around the "cloud trees" made the previous day using blocks, thin strips of bubble wrap, or paper strips.

In addition to the scenario, place a wire maze with beads that can be manipulated over the wires out on the floor (numerous sizes and varieties of these wire mazes are available in toy stores and from toy catalogs). The children at the symbolic level can pretend the beads are Fluffy on the path, and the children at the functional and sensorimotor levels can explore the movement of the beads along the wires.

Day 4 Add the clay and sponge porcupines and hippos made during Table Play the previous day to the miniature scenario so that the story can be enacted with the characters the children have made. You can take the part of one of the characters in order to stimulate the reenactment of the story. In addition, have the switch toys and the wire maze out on the floor.

Day 5   Repeat the miniature scenario. Add miniature marshmallows and small caps full of shaving cream to the scenario.

In addition, place switch toys (different ones, if possible) as well puzzles and books with pictures of different animals out on the floor. If possible, find books that have pictures of the animals represented on the puzzles. Encourage children to find and match pictures in the books to the pictures on the puzzles.

Day 1   Repeat the miniature scenario.

WEEK 2

Play Hungry Hungry Hippos. This is a fun game that most of the children will enjoy because it has few rules. (The four hungry hippos race to see who can eat the most marbles. Any child who can push a lever down will be able to play this game.) Puzzles and books of animals can be placed out on the floor for children to select if they choose not to play Hungry Hungry Hippos.

Jars of differing sizes (baby food jars to larger jars) are filled with things that make soft (not very noisy) sounds (e.g., paper strips, fabric, cotton balls) and things that make hard (noisy) sounds (e.g., beans, screws, marbles). These sound jars are placed out on the floor for the children to shake and compare. Facilitate their play by commenting on the sounds and encouraging the children to describe the sounds. Explain how noises can be hard and soft, just like objects can be hard and soft. Have soft and hard materials available so that when you listen to soft sounds you can feel the soft materials and when you listen to the hard sounds you can feel the hard materials.

Day 2   Repeat the miniature scenario and all of the previous day's activities. Change the white marbles in the Hungry Hungry Hippos game to marbles of different colors. At the end of the game, the children can count how many marbles of each color they have.

Day 3   Leave out the plastic characters, blocks, dollhouse, and so forth to role-play the story.

Add pick-up-sticks to the area to make the Pick-Up Fluffy's Quills game. Show the children how to try to pick up a stick without moving the other sticks. This is very difficult, so change the "no movement" of the other sticks rule. Encourage the children to pick up the "one on top." The goal should be to take turns and use a pincer grasp to pick up the stick as carefully as possible.

Place out "porcupine" balls (Jiggle Balls, battery-operated balls with plastic knobs sticking out of them that vibrate and bounce around the floor when switched on); these balls appeal to all levels of children. Compare the spikes on the ball to the quills on Fluffy. Have the children play a rolling back-and-forth game with another child. Children who crave sensory input will benefit from play with the vibrating ball.

Day 4   Place large, deep bowls on the floor in which you have placed boiled potatoes from the previous day's activity in the Science and Math Center. Give the children an "old fashioned" potato masher and let them go to it. (Having the bowls on the floor will allow the children to be over the potatoes so that they can exert more force in their mashing.) If desired, milk or water may be added to make mashing easier. The children will love watching the potatoes change to mush. (Don't worry if they taste some.) An electric mixer may also be used at the end, with supervision.

Hide the "porcupine" balls, and let the children find them by following the noise of the ball.

Day 5   Repeat playing Hungry Hungry Hippos.

Repeat the miniature scenario.

Texture tubs from the Sensory Area may be placed on the floor.

Play with the "porcupine" balls can continue. Let the children try to roll the ball toward a target of a rhinoceros. Also have mirrors available and let the children watch their faces in the mirror as they hold the vibrating ball to their cheeks. Describe the action of the ball and discuss how the ball feels.

Sensorimotor Level

1. Let the children at the sensorimotor level put animals or sensory objects in a container. They will enjoy making the objects disappear and then re-appear when they dump them out.

2. These children will enjoy activating animal switch toys. As the children learn how to turn on the toys, you can substitute toys with more complicated activating mechanisms. Some children may need toys with a simple switch pad.

3. Rolling a battery-operated "porcupine" ball will appeal to these children. The vibrations are beneficial for children who need increased sensory input as well. Encourage these children to roll the ball with a peer.

4. For these children, expand the number of actions on objects (model using different actions on objects to reduce perseveration, or repetition of the same action over and over). Encourage the ability to take a turn. You can do this by imitating the child's actions. When the child notices that you are doing what he or she is doing, the action will most likely be repeated. After several imitative turns, modify your action slightly to see if the child will imitate you.

5. Model sound production and label objects and actions for children at this level. Many of the sound-producing activities offer opportunities to make fun noises for the children to imitate.

6. Have several options available for these children to encourage making choices and to provide opportunities for the child to use varied actions.

Functional Level

1. For children at the functional level, you can expand their problem-solving skills by presenting switch toys, puzzles, and so forth. Encourage the children to figure out a way to start the toy, fix the puzzle, and so forth before providing a cue or prompt. Then provide visual cues to the children, pointing to the important components or providing minimal support. Increase support until the children can solve the problem independently.
2. Children at this level will need models and prompts while playing Hungry Hungry Hippos (e.g., "The hippos ate all the marbles," "I'm going to put mine back in the middle so they can eat again"). Encourage them to count the marbles that their hippo ate or identify the colors of the marbles.
3. Promote parallel play when these children are building the trees (use a peer as a model, if possible).
4. Relate the tree structure to the story for these children by adding props related to the story and showing them the pictures in the book. Using blocks as a tree structure involves symbolic play, and children at this level will need some support to see the relationship. They may imitate building but not have a goal in mind of making a tree.
5. Children at this level are just beginning to understand dramatic play. The miniature scenario will be more meaningful if realistic looking toys are used. For instance, you may want to add some toy trees in addition to the block trees.

Symbolic Level

1. Encourage children at the symbolic level to develop the concept of *rules* when playing Hungry Hungry Hippos or pick-up sticks. What is the appropriate sequence of play? Have them explain the rules to peers. Let them make up new game rules and explain those.
2. Have these children practice turn taking with a peer with all floor activities. Help them to understand that not all of the children know how to take turns and they can help teach the other children so that everyone can have fun. You can model how to cue a child for his or her turn and how to comment on the other child's actions.
3. Prompt higher level thought with these children (e.g., "My hippo ate five marbles. How many did yours eat?" "What else do you think we need in our story scene?").
4. Provide information for these children (e.g., "I don't think hippos really eat marbles. I think they eat plants"; "Rhinoceroses live in Africa").
5. Encourage children at this level to do more complex problem solving (e.g., "The batteries in this toy don't work. Let's figure out how to put in new ones"). Comment on their efforts and encourage them to think of alternative solutions.

6. The miniature scenario offers children at this level an opportunity to engage in dramatic play during which they can manipulate the interaction of characters. You may model this by assuming the role of one of the characters and initiating an interaction with the other characters (controlled by the children). Once the children have a story going, you can turn your character over to another child.
7. Encourage creative use of materials in making the miniature scenario. Let these children think of materials they could use for clouds, trees, a path, and so forth.

TABLE PLAY

Day 1   The children can make sandpaper porcupines. They can trace around their own or their peers' hands on a fine grade of sandpaper. Then they, or you, can cut out their drawings. When these are cut out, googly eyes (clear plastic eyes with a black piece inside that moves) can be glued on to finish the porcupines. Encourage the children to feel the texture of the sandpaper. Describe it as "rough," "scratchy," and "hard." Because the sandpaper is more difficult to cut than paper, cutting through it requires more pressure and control and provides additional pressure on the part of the child. Let the children do as much of the cutting independently as possible, providing only minimal support to allow them to cut successfully.

    Play Silly Faces Colorform game. This game lets children make funny faces. Encourage the children to try to make each other laugh (like Fluffy and Hippo) with their silly faces. Try to imitate the silly faces by using a hand mirror.

Day 2   The children can make sponge hippos or rhinoceroses with oval sponges and empty thread spools or bottle caps. Two empty thread spools or bottle caps can be glued onto the bottom of an upright oval sponge to make legs. Cut a notch out of the sponge on one side to make a mouth in the head (the head and body are together in the oval). Add eyes with a marker or glue on googly eyes. The hippos can be used as figures in the miniature scenario or glue a Popsicle stick on the bottom to make puppets.

    Continue to make sandpaper porcupines.

    Repeat the Silly Faces Colorform game.

Day 3   Make clay porcupine families. The children can roll balls of clay into which they can stick toothpicks (or straws or Tinker Toy sticks if they need larger objects to manipulate) to make clay porcupine families. Use the porcupines as little puppets. They can interact with the sponge hippos and rhinoceroses.

    Continue to make the sponge hippos and rhinoceroses.

Day 4   The children can make Styrofoam animal "characters" by adding different materials to Styrofoam balls, including bobby pins, spools, buttons, cotton balls, and other creative materials. Let their imaginations run wild. They can create and name their characters. Encourage the children to describe what they have made. What does their animal eat? Where does it sleep? Who is its friend? Write down their responses. The children can let their animals play together in the miniature scenario with Fluffy and Hippo.

    Continue to make clay porcupines.

Day 5   Repeat the previous day's activity. Display the animal characters the children have made with a dictated caption about their animal. Let the children "read" the description of their animal to the other children. Compare the animals that the children have made in terms of how they are alike and different. Encourage the children to ask each other questions about their animals. Asking questions is often difficult for children with special needs, so you and the other children may need to model or provide a sample question for the children to imitate.

Day 1   Have the children bring in a shoebox from home to make a miniature felt storyboard. (Make sure that you include this in one of the letters that you send home to the children's families.) Assist the children in cutting out a piece of felt to fit on the inside of the lid of the box. Let the children use crayons, markers, stickers, and so forth to decorate the outside of their box.

   Let the children put together the large puzzle from Blue's Clues—Big Easy Game on the table. Identify the soft or fluffy objects or hard or sharp items in the puzzle.

Day 2   Have the children trace and cut out characters or anything they want from the story from pieces of felt. Depending on each child's cutting skills, these may not actually resemble the real animals, but that is unimportant if the child is happy with the outcome. If he or she is not pleased, you can help "shape it up" by cutting it out a little better or by drawing an outline of the animal on the child's cutout shape. The child may want to glue a few toothpicks onto Fluffy for quills. An easy alternative to this more difficult cutting is to have the children cut a circular shape around a photocopied picture of the characters from the book. Glue a piece of cardboard to the back of the picture to make it more stable, and then glue a small piece of Velcro to the back of the cardboard.

   Have the easel set up with paint. Place pictures of a porcupine, a rhinoceros, and a hippopotamus next to the easel to provide an inspirational model.

   Repeat the Blue's Clues—Big Easy Game.

Day 3   Take the felt animals made the previous day, and have the children dip them in liquid starch and set them aside to dry. This will make them stiffer and easier to handle. (Obviously, do not do this with the paper alternatives!)

   Have the easel set up with markers. Keep the pictures of the animals near the easel. After a child draws a picture, you can label the picture with the child's words. If possible, obtain flawed matting boards from frame shops, and have the children help you mount the pictures for display.

   Have puzzles of jungle animals out for children to put together.

Day 4   Let the children act out the story with their felt storyboard boxes. The felt animals can be placed on the felt lid as the children describe what is happening. Encourage them to make up a new story or add to the story of Fluffy and

Hippo. What might the new friends do together? (If the pieces do not adhere well to the felt lid, glue a small piece of Velcro onto the back of the animal pieces.) Later, the pieces can be placed inside the box for storage.

Have a bowl full of pine cones and another full of googly eyes. The children can glue the eyes on the pine cones to make porcupines. Discuss the "head" and the "tail" of the porcupine, letting the children find the "fattest" or "biggest" part for the head and placement of the eyes and the "thinnest" or "smallest" part for the tail. Use the word "opposites" to describe these terms.

Day 5 The children can create clay or Play-Doh animals to which they can add pieces of pine cone, pipe cleaners, and so forth. Encourage the children to use a variety of materials. Help the children to think about all of the body parts and materials that could be used to represent those parts.

Sensorimotor Level

1. Place objects from the Floor Play area at the table for children at the sensorimotor level who need more stability.
2. Motivate children to explore and try new actions rather than emphasize a product outcome.
3. Show the children at this level how to attach the felt animals to the felt lid. The goal for them is not representational playing but rather seeing how the parts can be combined. They may also enjoy hiding the pieces in the box and finding them again. This encourages the development of object permanence (the memory that something exists even when not seen).
4. Substitute larger straws, dowels, or Tinker Toy sticks for these children to use when manipulating and poking clay.
5. Encourage the children at this level to feel the sandpaper. You may trace their hands. Point out their hands and the separate fingers. Although you may add eyes to the hands, these children will not understand the hands as representing porcupines. The sandpaper porcupines may be completed so they will look like porcupines to the other children and the children's families.
6. The goal for children at this level is to manipulate the various objects, combine objects, observe and imitate the actions of peers, and use sounds or words to comment on the objects and actions.

Functional Level

1. Although you should encourage sensory exploration in children at the functional level, begin to encourage meaningful action sequences during which the children perform a sequence of actions to accomplish a goal.

2. Keep activities to two to three steps so that these children can do them with little prompting or help.
3. Children at this level will not be able to accurately cut out an animal. Let them cut a piece of felt (of any shape). Then draw an animal figure on their felt piece with a marker. This will help children to see the piece as an animal they can attach to the board. These children may benefit from pieces made with pictures from the story, as they are more familiar. Encourage them to observe how their friends are using their felt pieces on the felt lid.
4. Encourage representational thinking (e.g., clay with toothpicks is a porcupine) in these children.
5. Expand these children's utterances to include verbs and descriptions.
6. Prompt conversations among these children by arranging the environment so that they need to request materials.
7. Pair these children with children at a lower level so that they can initiate, demonstrate, and take turns.

Symbolic Level

1. Encourage children at the symbolic level to make the characters and to act out the story. Prompt representation of not just characters but actions, feelings, and expansions or alterations of the story (e.g., "What did Fluffy and Hippo do next?").
2. Prompt these children to use the felt characters in the miniature scenario during Floor Play or in the Literacy Center for telling a story. This will enable the children to see that their artwork can be used in more than one context.
3. Picture charts of sequences (e.g., ball of clay + toothpicks = porcupine) are useful for these children. Use both pictures and words so that the children associate the words with the pictures and actions.
4. Encourage labeling and naming of creations by these children.
5. Let the children at this level help create the means for displaying the projects. You may want to combine them into mobiles or mount them in small boxes.
6. Encourage children at this level to think ahead about what they want to make; the components; and what they need to do first, second, and so forth.

WOODWORKING CENTER

This area is set up only for the first week. If desired, because of limited space, these activities could be substituted for some of the Science and Math Center activities. (*Note:* Supervision is especially important in this area. Do not let the children play unsupervised with real tools.)

Day 1   The children can experiment with putting different size nails and screws into wood and Styrofoam. They can measure the pieces of wood or Styrofoam with a ruler and with a measuring tape. Using a screwdriver and using a hammer require different processes. Let the children try both. Label the tools the children are using, and describe their actions. Provide hard hats and goggles to increase safety, motivate the children, and encourage representational play.

WEEK 1

Day 2   The children can continue to experiment with the screws and nails and the tools. Some children may choose to make a bed for Fluffy out of the wood and nails. Provide a picture chart of the process. They will need to measure and cut the pieces. Provide a vise to hold the pieces together. Duct tape can be used to help hold the pieces together. Styrofoam can also be used and fastened together with tape. It does not matter if the bed is symmetrical or even. The process of making something and then using it is what counts! Make sure a toy porcupine squeeze toy or other porcupine is available to use in the bed or house.

Day 3   Children continue to work on making a bed for Fluffy by nailing together the pieces of wood, by taping pieces of Styrofoam together, or by using wood glue to fasten the pieces. Some children will just experiment with putting the pieces together without trying to make something of them. Do not worry if the project does not resemble anything real!

Day 4   The children can continue working on Fluffy's bed. They can cut foam rubber (measure first) for the mattress and cut a square of material for the cover for the bed. Even if a bed structure was not completed, the children can experiment with combining the boards, Styrofoam, foam rubber, and cloth.

Day 5   The children finish Fluffy's bed. The children can paint the bed and then add the mattress and covers. Then Fluffy can be added to the bed. (Use the clay Fluffy made during Table Play.) Let the children plan what is needed and the sequence for the actions.

If desired, the activities of Week 1 can be extended so that the children can continue to experiment with the tools and building. Add new picture charts, and let the children build a tree, a house, a path, a chair, and so forth.

Sensorimotor Level

1. Substitute plastic hammers and peg boards or plastic hammers with real wood for children at the sensorimotor level.
2. Make noises and model words for these children (e.g., "bang, bang"; "in," "out").
3. Children at this level will try to imitate the gestures of their peers. Have them watch what their friends are doing. Assist with physical support only when needed.
4. Let the children at this level put the animals into the bed.

Functional Level

1. Let children at the functional level explore the use of the real tools. Building "something" is not important. Name the tools and discuss the actions made by the tools.
2. Have these children follow three-step sequences (e.g., find a board, find a nail and hold it to the wood, and pound in the nail).
3. Encourage these children to count the nails, screws, boards, and so forth.
4. Assist these children in putting the wood in a vise and turning the screw. Then let the children experiment with the vise and wood themselves.
5. Use visual cues to demonstrate for these children rather than relying on verbal directions. Use short sentences to communicate.
6. Pair children at this level with children at the symbolic level, as children at the symbolic level will model use of vocabulary and demonstrate appropriate actions with the tools and materials.

Symbolic Level

1. Children at the symbolic level can plan, problem-solve, and build a bed for Fluffy. Encourage them to do all of this by asking open-ended questions (e.g., "Let's think. What do you think we should do first?" "What can we do to hold these together?").
2. Help the children at this level follow the pictures on the picture chart.
3. These children can measure and write down numbers. Help them to read a simple ruler with only inch marks.
4. Talk with these children about "equal" lengths and the "same" sides of the bed.

5. Discuss the shapes of the materials and make comparisons of sizes.
6. Encourage the children to classify the tools by function (e.g., "Tools or materials that hold things together," "Tools that put screws and nails in and take them out").
7. Encourage children at this level to do higher level problem solving using analytical and divergent thinking. Rather than demonstrate the answer to the problem, help the children to analyze the characteristics of the problem and brainstorm solutions.
8. Encourage children at the symbolic level to evaluate their efforts. For some this will be merely having an opinion as to whether they like their product. Others can be encouraged to analyze and think about what they like best about their product and what they would like to improve.

OUTDOOR PLAY

Day 1   Play Red Rover, Red Rover, We Want Fluffy to Come Over (a modification of the traditional Red Rover game). Have the children sit in rows across from each other. Put a feather boa (or long, silky scarf) around the neck of one child (he or she becomes Fluffy). The group of children on the opposite side from Fluffy yell "Red Rover, Red Rover, We Want Fluffy to Come Over." Fluffy then moves to the other side (runs, walks, crawls, rolls, or moves any way he or she wants). Fluffy then gives the boa to another child, and the other side repeats the sequence. Encourage the children to move in funny ways and try to make the other children laugh like Fluffy and Hippo in the story.

Free play.

Day 2   On a nature walk, the children can look for "hard" objects. You can carry egg cartons or a bucket for the children to use to put the objects in. The children can decide if the object goes in the "hard" bucket (e.g., rocks, sticks). On leaving and entering the building, the children can follow a winding rope to a surprise (the bucket on the way out and a bag with the snack in it on the way back). When you return from the walk, sit in a group and examine the objects found by the children. Let the children pass the objects around, name what they found, and discuss how they feel. The children can then sort the objects into piles of things that are alike in some way.

Free play.

Day 3   Take another nature walk. This time, have the children look for "soft" objects. The children can place "soft" objects, such as grass and leaves, into an egg carton or a bucket.

The shape path to be used the next day on Fluffy's path in the Dramatic Play: Theme Area can be put out for the children to walk on or jump on (or roll over in a wheelchair) as they leave and enter the classroom. (These shapes are made from heavy colored paper and are made by staff prior to class.)

Free play.

Day 4   In the story, Fluffy discovers that his quills puncture an umbrella. This fun activity will let the children know it is better to have an umbrella that does not have holes in it. Several children are given umbrellas, and several other children are given spray bottles filled with water. The children with the spray bottles go after the children with umbrellas who protect themselves from the spray by raising their umbrellas.

In another area, the rope path in and out of the classroom can be used again, with the children walking one foot in front of the other beside the rope. Let the children take turns rearranging the rope into new shapes to follow.

Free play.

Day 5

Go for a walk to look for pine cones or other "prickly" things. The pine cones will be saved to be used at the Table Play area to make porcupines. Talk about where pine cones come from and look for their origin.

Take a heavy blanket out to the playground and let the children roll around on it like Fluffy and Hippo. Then wrap two children up together, and swing them, with one adult on each end of the blanket. Let the children count to 10 as you swing. Then unwrap them and let two more children get wrapped up and swing. Continue as long as your arms hold out or until the children get tired.

Free play.

Day 1

Hide the porcupines outside that were made by the children at Table Play earlier that day (hide most in fairly obvious places). The children then find them and bring them back to you. (Keep track of where they were found so that all of them will be accounted for.) The children can help count them and determine how many are left to find.

Take the barrel (see Motor Area) outside, and let the children roll a friend inside the barrel across the grass.

Free play.

Day 2

Set up a tricycle obstacle course path outside. Some of the children maneuver this course, and some can play on the outdoor equipment. Take the gym mat outside and let the children tumble and roll on it, like Fluffy and Hippo. Repeat the spray bottles and umbrella play.

The children can exit and enter the building walking like a hippopotamus (all fours), a giraffe (hands clasped high above the head), or an elephant (bent over with hands clasped and swinging back and forth).

Free play.

Day 3

Have the children move outside and inside on the numbered circles that were made for the path in the Dramatic Play: Theme Area. You can identify specific numbers for children to walk on or let the children choose on which circle to step.

Play Fluffy Says (like Simon Says). The children can pretend to be hippos, and Fluffy can tell them funny things to do to make them laugh. For instance, Fluffy can make a silly face for Hippo to imitate or can move in a silly way. After two tries to make everyone laugh, another child can be Fluffy.

Free play.

Day 4   Bring the ladder outside, and let the children walk over it in different ways when it is flat on the ground. They did this in the Dramatic Play: Theme Area when it was Fluffy's path, and they will probably remember some of the ways they walked down it. Add backward and sideways movements for those who can maneuver well enough.

Play Fluffy, Fluffy, Hippo (just like Duck, Duck, Goose).

Free play.

Day 5   Bring the big paper circles outside that were used for the path in the Dramatic Play: Theme Area. Use large dowels or sticks to connect the dots in different ways so that the children can follow the path between the sticks. Let the children rearrange the circles and sticks to make new patterns. You and the children can suggest different ways to move down the path.

Bring the Blue's Clues—Big Easy Game outside for the children to play.

Free play. (See Chapter 4 in the *Teacher's Guide* for overall considerations when individualizing for children with motor disabilities.)

Sensorimotor Level

1. Children at this level can be included in all of the activities in some way. Even though they will not understand the purpose of a game or activity, they will benefit from involvement at their own level of understanding. For example, while playing Red Rover, Red Rover, We Want Fluffy to Come Over, the children at this level will enjoy feeling the feather boa. You and the rest of the class can entice the children at this level to move to the other side by calling their names or holding up a favorite toy.

2. You may need to assist these children's movements for some of the activities. When providing assistance, make sure these children are also contributing to the movement efforts so that they benefit from using the various muscle groups.

3. Let these children feel the hard and prickly and soft objects found on the nature walk. Instead of labeling the characteristics, label the object (e.g., "Look at the pretty *rock*").

4. For the umbrella activity, let the children at this level experience both roles, being sprayed and spraying others. You may need to assist with holding the umbrella or helping to squeeze the spray bottle. Look for squirt guns or bottles that are easily activated so that these children can squeeze them independently.

5. When the children are walking on the shapes, point out to these children what is happening. Stand or sit the children on a shape and let them notice that they are in a defined space.

6. Use simple words to describe to these children what other children are doing. This will help build their language comprehension of action words.

Functional Level

1. Children at this level will understand the actions (e.g., running) in a game but will not understand the sequence or rules of the game. You will need to prompt these children when it is their turn to run. Explain the cue that tells them when it is their turn.
2. On the nature walk, children at this level will benefit from repetition of concepts. Hold a "hard" object next to a "soft" object (e.g., a rock next to grass), and label each appropriately. Let the child feel the objects as they say the descriptive words. These more abstract concepts are learned only after repeated exposure to concrete examples.
3. These children will love the umbrella game. Encourage them to take turns with the roles of spraying and being sprayed. Demonstrate how the umbrella keeps them "dry."
4. Hide pine cones in easy places for these children. Have a place for them to bring and deposit the pine cones. This will encourage them to establish a three-step pattern—find, bring, and place.
5. Encourage children at this level to imitate the actions of their peers, particularly for actions that require children at this level to engage in motor planning. Use verbal mediation and physical manipulation to assist the children in getting their bodies to do what they want them to.
6. Point to and name the colors, shapes, and numbers on the paper path as these children walk on them.

Symbolic Level

1. Children at the symbolic level are just beginning to understand rules of games. Help them to understand the sequence of play and the cues to the next step. Encourage them to explain the steps to their friends. In this way you can monitor their understanding of the games.
2. On the nature walk, you can help children at this level analyze the characteristics of the objects they find. Point out that an object can have more than one characteristic. It has a color and a shape, for instance. An object can be "hard" and "rough" or "hard" and "smooth." These observations will facilitate the child's developing understanding of multiple attributes.
3. Encourage children at this level to take turns as the water "squirter" and the "squirtee." (They may prefer to just be the one doing the squirting.) Discuss what would happen if the umbrella had holes in it like Fluffy's. You may be able to find an old umbrella that you can puncture for this experiment.
4. Tell children at this level that they are special detectives who are to look for the pine cones that cannot be seen. Point out a pine cone that is visible and explain that finding the ones you can see is the job of the assistant detectives.
5. Children at the symbolic level can be encouraged to follow the paper path using color, shape, or number as the guide.

SNACK

Day 1 Oral motor: Have the children make "soft" sounds (e.g., "mmm," "ttt," "sss") and "hard" sounds (e.g., "kkk," "ddd"). Identify animals that might make a particular sound (e.g., a woodpecker would make a hard sound, a snake would make a soft sound). Each child can choose an animal and make the animal sound. The others can then decide if the sound is "hard" or "soft."

Snack: Serve soft and prickly "porcupines" and juice to drink.

SOFT AND PRICKLY PORCUPINES

Large marshmallows (or a piece of fruit such as a chunk of banana or a section of orange)
Pretzel sticks
   Give each child 10 pretzels (they can count them out). Have them poke the pretzels into a marshmallow (or piece of fruit) to make a porcupine. They can then eat the pretzels one at a time and finish with the marshmallow for dessert!

Day 2 Oral motor: Have the children make their favorite animal sounds and have the others imitate.

Snack: Make and serve soft and crunchy trail mix. Serve water to drink.

SOFT AND CRUNCHY TRAIL MIX

Raisins
Peanuts
Chocolate chips
Pine nuts or sunflower seeds
   Have the children dump all of the ingredients into a bowl and take turns mixing it up.

Have the children find the "soft" ingredient and the "hard" ingredients.

Day 3 Oral motor: Have the children wash their hands and faces, particularly their mouths, with a rough, wet washcloth. Have them pat their faces dry with a soft, dry cloth. Talk about the textures of both. Use different motions with the cloth to give different types of input (e.g., some hard, some soft, some rubbing, some patting). Use the words "hard," "soft," "rough," and so forth to describe the actions.

Snack: Serve soft bananas and crunchy carrots. Let each child peel a carrot (prewashed) with a vegetable peeler. Give each child a banana to peel and have them compare the two (e.g., hard, soft; crunchy, smooth). Have milk to drink.

Day 4   Oral motor: The children can choose their favorite animal and make the noise that animal makes. Sing "Can you do this? Can you do this? Mr. Hippo, Mr. Hippo?" (to the tune of "Frère Jacques") and accompany with actions. Let one child make faces, body movements, or gestures, and have other children imitate. Do the Number Actions fingerplay.

Snack: Serve crunchy celery with soft peanut butter. Have the children use plastic knives to spread peanut butter on the celery. Talk about which is hard and crunchy and which is soft and smooth. Have juice to drink.

Day 5   Oral motor: Sing "Did You Ever See a Porcupine?" Use funny facial movements for the children to imitate in the song.

Snack: Serve crunchy granola with soft yogurt or whipped cream. Let each child pour the granola into his or her bowl. Then let each child scoop a spoonful of whipped cream (made in the Science and Math Center) or yogurt on top of the granola. Again, talk about the textures as you taste each separately and then together. Have water to drink.

Day 1   Oral motor: Make "soft" (e.g., "ffff," "shh," "hhh") and "hard" (e.g., "ggg"; "br, br, br"; "ddd") sounds. Repeat singing "Did You Ever See a Porcupine?" Let the children make up the faces to imitate.   **WEEK 2**

Snack: Make and serve chocolate clouds. Make the chocolate clouds before going outdoors so that they will have time to cool and the chocolate can firm up. (If desired, the activity of making the chocolate clouds can take place in the Science and Math Center earlier in the day.) Make a simple picture chart to show the procedures.

CHOCOLATE CLOUDS

6-oz. package of chocolate chips
Marshmallows
1 package of coconut
   Melt the package of chocolate chips on top of the double boiler. Have the children use fondue forks or regular forks to dip their marshmallows in the chocolate and then roll the marshmallow in the coconut and set on a plate to cool. Have milk to drink.

Day 2   Oral motor: Integrate the concepts of *rough* and *soft* into the oral-motor activity. Give each child a rough, wet washcloth to wash their mouths (with a circular rubbing motion), and then a soft, dry cloth to dry their mouths (with a patting motion). Talk about "rough," "soft," "wet," "dry," "rub," and "pat."

Do the Number Actions fingerplay while holding up the appropriate number of fingers.

Snack: Serve oatmeal with cinnamon and apples. Use the oatmeal and apples from the Science and Math Center. Have the children who did the "hard" and "soft" experiments in the Science and Math Center show the others what the oatmeal and apples looked like before being cooked and tell what they did before cooking them. Then the other children can combine the oatmeal and apples and add cinnamon (which everyone can smell) and a little sugar. The mixture can be reheated in the microwave and served in small bowls for snack. Have milk to put on the oatmeal and to drink.

Day 3

Oral motor: Making animal faces and sounds is fun and works many facial muscles. The children can pick different animals to try, including a porcupine smacking its lips, a rhinoceros opening very wide and closing its mouth, a fish sucking in the corners of the mouth and then opening and closing the lips, and other animals that the children choose.

Snack: Make applesauce so that "hard" and "crunchy" becomes "soft" and "lumpy."

BLENDER APPLESAUCE

Apples (one per child)
½ teaspoon of water per apple
1 teaspoon of sugar per apple
Cinnamon

Have the children help you prepare the apples. The children can help wash the apples. You can then peel, core, and quarter the apples, with the children assisting whenever possible. Each child can be given a slice of apple to look at, break, smell, and feel. Talk about how the slice is crunchy when they bite into it. The children can then add the water and sugar to the blender. Add the apples one at a time, and blend before adding another. You can have the children describe what is happening to the apples as they watch. Have apple juice to drink. Discuss how the flavor and the texture of the apple juice are different from those of applesauce.

Day 4

Oral motor: Do the Number Actions fingerplay.

Snack: Serve French fries and mashed potatoes with water to drink. Show what mashed potatoes look like, and have the children who made them in the Science and Math Center explain what they did to prepare the potatoes. Add a little butter and salt to the mashed potatoes, and finish mixing. First let each child try the hand masher and then an electric hand mixer until the potatoes are creamy. Let each child who is able hold the mixer for a few seconds. Discuss the texture. Serve each child a small portion to taste.

Open the frozen French fries. Make sure they are microwavable. Again, show the children an uncooked, frozen French fry. Then show them the mashed potatoes. Let them each look at and touch a frozen French fry. Talk about "cold" and "crunchy." Cook the French fries (untouched) in the microwave and serve. Discuss what happens to the fries when they are cooked. Discuss how they are now "hot" and "soft."

Day 5   Oral motor: Repeat making porcupine lip smacks and hippo yawns. Sing "If You're Happy and You Know It." Add 1) "If you're happy and you know it, make a smile . . .," 2) "If you're sad and you know it, make a frown . . .," 3) "If you're silly and you know it, make a face . . .," and 4) "If you're grouchy and you know it, stick out your tongue. . . ."

Snack: Serve soft and crunchy vegetables and dip with milk to drink.

DIP

16-ounce carton of sour cream
1 package of powdered dip mix or one carton of already-made dip (any flavor)
Vegetables (use a variety, such as tomatoes, cucumbers, cauliflower, broccoli, and
    carrots)
   If making the dip, follow the directions on the package of dip, allowing the children to take turns mixing. Let the children help wash and cut or break off the vegetable pieces. Then have each child select several vegetable pieces and some dip on a small plate. Discuss which is soft and which is crunchy. They can then dip their veggies and eat them.

Sensorimotor Level

1. Oral-motor activities are important for children at the sensorimotor level who are learning to talk. Activities that encourage them to control the movements of their lips, tongue, teeth, and jaw will give them practice needed for formulating sounds and words. Demonstrate the sounds and mouth movements for children at this level in a slow, exaggerated way.
2. Children at this level can benefit from experiencing various textures and consistencies of food. Hard foods require more movement of the tongue, teeth, and jaw. Encourage children to taste all of the various foods. Some children may need to be introduced to hard foods more slowly.
3. Encourage these children to imitate songs and fingerplays.
4. Involve children at this level in helping to make the snacks, serve them to their peers, and eat independently. Provide only as much support as is needed for the children to be able to be independent.
5. Use adaptive utensils as needed to aid independence.

Functional Level

1. All of the points for children at the sensorimotor level apply to children at the functional level as well.
2. Children at this level can be encouraged to do two to three steps in making the snack. Help them to look at the picture charts and imitate their

peers. They will benefit from concrete demonstrations more than from pictures, but the pictures and words on the chart can help move these children into a higher level of symbolic understanding.

3. Help the children at this level to learn the names of the various foods.
4. Give "wait time" (pause for the children to respond) when doing the songs and fingerplays so that the children at this level have time to process the next phrase or action.
5. Have these children compare the colors and shapes of foods.
6. Count the items being served to promote one-to-one correspondence with these children.

Symbolic Level

1. Children at the symbolic level can become involved in discussions comparing and contrasting the foods, textures, tastes, consistencies, and so forth.
2. Encourage these children to plan for how many plates, cups, and so forth are needed for the day.
3. Children at this level can lead the group in following the picture chart and making the snack. Facilitate matching the pictures and words on the chart to the action sequence.
4. You can enhance the vocabulary of children at this level having discussions about categories (fruits, vegetables) to encourage classification.
5. Discuss with these children different ways to describe the same thing (color, shape, texture, etc.) to encourage identification of multiple attributes of objects.
6. Talk about the flavors these children like and dislike and why.
7. When making snacks, help children at this level to think about the sequence of activities by having them describe what they are doing, what is happening, and why.

HOW TO INVOLVE FAMILIES

Families can be involved in the story of *A Porcupine Named Fluffy* in many ways. A week or so before the book is read, send caregivers a letter letting them know what you will be reading. Include with the letter a list of needed items that they may be able to help supply, the vocabulary list from the beginning of the module, and the planning sheets from the beginning of the module. You can also let the families know some of the activities you will be doing and some things they might try at home. The following is a sample of the first letter:

Date

Dear families,

We're getting ready to start a new book called *A Porcupine Named Fluffy*, by Helen Lester. This is a great book with funny illustrations that will provide us with lots of opportunities to talk about things that are soft and things that are prickly or hard. We'll be acting out the story, experimenting with different materials, and making fun art projects. You may want to check this book out of your local library or even buy a copy at a local bookstore. Your child will then be able to share with you more about what is happening in school. You can also reinforce what is being learned at school by using the same book and concepts that we're using in school.

Many of the activities we will be doing in class will use things you may have around the house. Please see if you have any of the following to spare. We would appreciate your sharing with us. (Please be sure to label all of the items that you want to be returned.)

- Angel hair (that white "stuff" we use for spider webs at Halloween)
- Bobby pins
- Bottle caps, corks
- Bubble wrap
- Cotton balls
- Fabric remnants
- Flannel pieces
- Magazines or catalogs with pictures of animals
- Old umbrellas
- Pine cones
- Potatoes
- Rope
- Sandpaper
- Shoeboxes
- Sponges
- Spray water bottles
- Styrofoam pieces

- Tennis balls
- Toothpicks
- Wood chips and small pieces of wood, including balsa wood

During the next 2 weeks, we will also be using many new words (a list is attached). Some children will be learning them in sign language, some will be learning them in words, and some will even begin to read and write the words. Depending on what your child is ready for, you can use these words at home and support your child's use of them.

We are going to be doing many activities to explore the concepts of "fluffy," "soft," "prickly," and "hard." Some of these activities will entail messy substances, such as shaving cream. You may want to send in a bathing suit or extra old clothes for your child to wear during these activities. Anything we use, however, will be washable! You can use these same words at home when drying your child off with a fluffy towel, walking on a soft carpet or rug, sleeping on a fluffy pillow, eating hard carrots or prickly pretzels, and so forth. It's great when your child can hear you using the same words we use at school, only applied to different items found at home. That will help your child learn how to understand and use these words in many ways.

We are also going to be making felt board theaters out of old shoeboxes, so we can tell you the story with our felt pieces. Please see if you have an old shoebox you can send in to class. It will come back to you as a decorated box with a felt board on the lid and felt board characters from the story inside it. We hope you will have fun telling the story of Fluffy to each other with the felt board theater. As always, feel free to join our play and learning.

Thank you!

Sincerely,

Prior to the second week, send another letter home to the family to report on the past week's activities and introduce the coming week. The following is a sample letter:

Date

Dear families,

We have been having a lot of fun experimenting with things that are hard and soft and smooth and prickly. You may have seen your child feeling, lying on, jumping on, or even trying to wear a pillow! That's because in our book, Fluffy tries to be a pillow in order to become fluffy. We've also been experimenting with cotton balls, bubbles, spaghetti (before and after it is cooked), and shaving cream. You might want to include bubble bath and some utensils, such as spoons and a whisk, in your child's bath. Fingerpainting with shaving cream (on a plastic place mat or on the side of the tub) is also fun. Tub foam is also available at most discount department stores.

Some of us have been making things stick together with tape, glue, Velcro, staples, and nails. Don't be surprised if your child wants to continue some of this experimentation at home. If you can provide a space and paper and tape, that would be great! Brothers and sisters can join in, too. These activities are helping the children to use their fine motor skills as well as work on ways to solve problems. We like to let the children experiment with all of the materials and then show them how the tools can be used to fasten things together.

Some of us are painting pictures of the story, and some of us are telling and writing stories. We'll be sending home some of your child's work soon. We are also making interesting art projects. If your child starts tracing around his or her hand, don't panic. That's a porcupine! You may want to get your child to tell you about it. You can write down what your child says on a piece of paper. Read back your child's words for him or her to hear. You might be surprised to hear your child trying to "read" the words to you as well. Have fun!

The children will also be making the felt board theaters from the shoeboxes you sent in last week. When your child brings the decorated shoebox back home, look inside for felt characters. These can be stuck on the lid so that you and your child can tell the story of Fluffy.

Also, on Monday of this week we will be making slime. You may want to send in a bathing suit or old clothes so that good clothing won't get slimed! (It does, however, wash out.)

Have fun—we are!

Sincerely,

MORE SUGGESTIONS

Books

(*Note:* Titles listed below that are preceded by an asterisk are similar to the storybook featured in this module and may be your most appropriate substitutes with modifications if you are unable to locate the recommended storybook.)

Asche, F. (1997). *Moonbear's pet.* New York: Simon & Schuster, Books for Young Readers.

Carle, E. (1998). *The mixed-up chameleon.* New York: HarperCollins.

*Davoll, B. (1996). *The problem with prickles.* Chicago: Moody Press.

George, J.C. (1998). *Rhino romp.* New York: Disney Enterprises, Inc.

Hague, M. (1996). *The perfect present.* New York: Morrow Junior Books.

*Kaska, K. (1997). *Don't laugh Joe.* New York: G.P. Putnam's Sons.

Keller, H. (1991). *Horace.* New York: Greenwillow Books.

Kraus, L. (1977). *Leo the late bloomer.* New York: Windmill Books.

Meddaugh, S. (1996). *Martha blah blah.* Boston: Houghton Mifflin.

Trapani, I. (1992). *What am I? An animal guessing game.* Danvers, MA: Whispering Coyote Press.

Waddell, M. (1991). *The happy hedgehog band.* Cambridge, MA: Candlewick Press.

Woody. (1998). *If I were an animal.* Brookfield, CT: Millbrook Press.

Fingerplays, Songs, and Games

NUMBER ACTIONS

Hold up the right number of fingers. Let one child make faces, body movements, or gestures and have other children imitate.

Number 1, wiggle your tongue
Number 2, touch your shoe
Number 3, show your teeth
Number 4, show even more
Number 5, blink your eye
Number 6, lick your lips
Number 7, look up to heaven
Number 8, make your tongue straight
Number 9, make this sign (wave)
Number 10, do it again!

DID YOU EVER SEE A PORCUPINE?
(Sung to the tune of "Did You Ever See a Lassie?")

Did you ever see a porcupine,
A porcupine, a porcupine,
Did you ever see a porcupine go this way,
Go this way and that way,
And this way and that way,
Did you ever see a porcupine go this way and that way?

IF I WERE A PORCUPINE

If I were a porcupine,
[Hold hand up with finger spread like quills.]

I would be so glad
[Push corners of mouth up into a smile.]

To have a hippo as my friend
[Puff out cheeks.]

I'd never more be sad.
[Push corners of mouth down into a frown.]

We would always smile.
[Smile.]

We would always giggle.
[Giggle.]

We would rest a little while,
[Place head on hands as if sleeping.]

Then smile and laugh and wiggle!
[Do all three.]

MR. PORCUPINE

Porcupine ate until he was full,
[Make hands into the shape of a ball.]

And then he fell asleep in a little ball.
[Clasp hands with fingers intertwined.]

His friend sneaked up and gave a shout,
[Make a loud noise through your folded hands.]

Porcupine jumped, and his quills popped out!
[Jump up, open fingers on clasped hands so that they stand up straight.]

THE QUILLS OF THE PORCUPINE

I have ten porcupine quills
They all belong to me.
[Hold up ten fingers.]

I can make them do things.
Do you want to see?

I can shut them up tight
[Close fists.]

Or open them wide.
[Spread the fingers wide.]

I can put them together
[Hands together as in prayer.]

Or make them all hide.
[Put hands behind back.]

I can make them jump high
[Raise hands high.]

Or make them go low.
[Put hands down at the side.]

I can fold them up quietly
[Fold hands and place them in your lap.]

And sit just so.
[Sit with hands in lap.]

(Adapted from Cole, J., & Calmenson, S. [1991]. *The eentsy, weentsy spider: Finger-plays and action rhymes* [pp. 16–17]. New York: Mulberry Books.)

FLUFFY

When Fluffy is sleeping, he lies very still,
[Place two fists together to make a ball.]

But when he's excited, up pop his quills!
[Pop up all 10 fingers.]

When he is playing, his quills lie down,
[Clasp hands with fingers crossed.]

And when he is sad, his face makes a frown.
[Make frowning face.]

He wants to be fluffy like a cloud,
[Smile broadly.]

And he wants to make Hippo laugh out loud!
[Tickle your neighbor and laugh.]

"Animal Action" (I and II). (1987). In *Songs for creative movement*. Los Angeles: CBS/Fox Playhouse Video Youngheart Records.

"Willoughby, Wallaby, Woo." (1976). In *Singable songs for the very young*. Hollywood, CA: A & M Records, Inc.

Blue's Clues—Big Easy Game (University Games Corporation)

Elefun (Hasbro, Inc.)

Hungry Hungry Hippos (Milton Bradley)

My First Board Games (Otto Maier Verlag Ravensburg, Ravensburger, Germany)

No Peeking (Otto Maier Verlag Ravensburg, Ravensburger, Germany)

The Opposites Game (Otto Maier Verlag Ravensburg, Ravensburger, Germany)

Silly Faces Colorform (University Games Corporation)

Things in My House (Otto Maier Verlag Ravensburg, Ravensburger, Germany)

Software

Art center. (1993). San Mateo, CA: Creative Wonders.

Blue's ABC time activities. (1998). Woodinville, WA: Humongous Entertainment.

Cyberboogie! With Sharon, Lois & Bram. (1994). Park Ridge, NJ: Ehrlich Multimedia.

Fantastic word gizmo. (1999). Columbus, OH: Ohio Distinctive Software.

Hello Kitty: Big fun shapes and numbers. (1994). San Francisco: Big Top Productions.

If you give a mouse a cookie. (1995). New York: HarperCollins Interactive.

ODS amazing art corner. (1999). Columbus, OH: Ohio Distinctive Software.

Professor Eggword's discovery. (1999). Columbus, OH: Ohio Distinctive Software.

Richard Scarry's busy town reading. (1997). Mountain View, CA: Paramount Digital Entertainment.

WiggleWork® story pack 1. (1994). New York: Scholastic New Media.

WiggleWork® story pack 2. (1995). New York: Scholastic New Media.

ORDER FORM

READ, PLAY, AND LEARN! STORYBOOK ACTIVITIES FOR YOUNG CHILDREN
The Transdisciplinary Play-Based Curriculum from Toni Linder

Please send me the following:

_____ **Teacher's Guide** / Stock # 4005 / $45.00

_____ **Module Collection 1**
Stock # 4013 / $125.00

The Kissing Hand, by Audrey Penn
Somebody and the Three Blairs, by Marilyn Tolhurst
Picking Apples & Pumpkins,
   by Amy and Richard Hutchings
*The Little Old Lady Who Was Not Afraid
   of Anything*, by Linda Williams
The Knight and the Dragon, by Tomie dePaola
Night Tree, by Eve Bunting
Abiyoyo, by Pete Seeger
The Snowy Day, by Ezra Jack Keats

_____ **Module Collection 2**
Stock # 4021 / $125.00

A Porcupine Named Fluffy, by Helen Lester
The Three Little Javelinas, by Susan Lowell
First Flight, by David McPhail
Franklin Has a Sleepover, by Paulette
   Bourgeois and Brenda Clark
Friends, by Helme Heine
The Rainbow Fish, by Marcus Pfister
The Three Billy Goats Gruff, by Janet Stevens
A Rainbow of Friends, by P.K. Hallinan

ADDITIONAL TRANSDISCIPLINARY PLAY-BASED RESOURCES

Transdisciplinary Play-Based Assessment uses a play-based process with accompanying Observation Guidelines to assess a child's abilities and learning styles. Intervention guidelines in the companion volume, *Transdisciplinary Play-Based Intervention*, help individualize instruction to match each child's developmental level and personal characteristics. Forms to use with TPBA and TPBI are sold separately. Two training videotapes, developed by Toni W. Linder, are also available.

_____ **Transdisciplinary Play-Based Assessment** / Stock # 1626 / $44.00
_____ **Transdisciplinary Play-Based Intervention** / Stock # 1308 / $49.95
_____ Order **TPBA** and **TPBI** as a **set** / Stock # OLIN / $83.95
_____ **Transdisciplinary Play-Based Assessment and Intervention: Child Program Summary Forms**
   Stock # 1634 / $27.00 (pkg. of 5 tablets)
_____ **And You Thought They Were Just Playing** / Stock # 2223 / $175.00 / VHS videotape / 65 min.
_____ **Observing Kassandra** / Stock # 2665 / $169.00 / VHS videotape / 50 min.

_____ Bill my institution (purchase order must be attached)

_____ Payment enclosed (make checks payable to Brookes Publishing Co.)

____ VISA   ____ MC   ____ AMEX Credit Card #: _____ Exp. date: _____

Signature (needed for all credit card purchases): _____

Daytime telephone: _____

Name: _____

Address: _____

City/State/ZIP: _____

Maryland orders add 5% sales tax.

Photocopy order form and send to: Brookes Publishing Co., P.O. Box 10624, Baltimore, MD 21285-0624

FAX (410) 337-8539; call toll-free (8 A.M.–5 P.M. ET) (800) 638-3775; or order on-line at **www.brookespublishing.com**

Yours to review for 30 days, risk-free. Contact Customer Service for more information on Brookes Publishing's return policy.
Prices subject to change without notice. Prices may be higher outside the United States.   Source Code: BA18